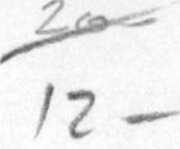

A BIBLIOGRAPHY OF SCOTTISH POETS
FROM STEVENSON TO 1974

Compiled with an Introduction
by Duncan Glen

With a Preface by Hugh MacDiarmid

Preston, Akros Publications, 1974

First published 1974
Akros Publications
14 Parklands Avenue, Penwortham,
Preston, Lancashire.
© Compilation and Introduction Duncan Glen 1974
© Preface C. M. Grieve 1974
Printed in Great Britain by
Lloyds Printers of Blackburn Limited

COMPILER'S NOTE

In compiling this bibliography of Scottish poets from Stevenson I have had to be selective to some extent although I have not excluded "known" poets of the past or present because I think poorly of their work. There are, however, many local, or occasional, or one-volume, or what I think of as "bit part" poets whom I have read but decided not to include. Some of these poets who are still writing will, I hope, go on to prove me wrong by producing volumes with poems of lasting worth.

This is a bibliography of books and pamphlets and of concrete poetry publications, and so poets who have contributed only to magazines or newspapers and whose poems have yet to be collected in book form do not appear. One of the things that has emerged from compiling this bibliography is that the young poets of Scotland have recently been quite surprisingly well catered for by small Scottish publishers (including the exiled "Scottish" publishers of this bibliography); the greater problem is for established poets who wish to have larger volumes of poems published although it is also surprising how many of these are now getting into print. Any list that I can give here of poets who have yet to have their work collected in book form can only be a list of those that I think already have a body of work requiring collection: Frederic Lindsay, David Angus and William Findlay who often write in Scots; Jean Milton and Alan Spence who write in English; and some of the Gaelic poets mentioned by Hugh MacDiarmid in his "Preface" whom Derick Thomson lists in his *An Introduction to Gaelic Poetry,* pp. 265-266.

This is a bibliography of *Scottish* poets although it is not easy to draw a line in that not all the poets I have included were born in Scotland (one thinks immediately of Sydney Goodsir Smith born in Wellington, New Zealand, and of Ian Hamilton Finlay born in Nassau, Bahamas) and some, such as George MacBeth, although born in Scotland may seem to belong more to London than to anywhere in Scotland. On the other hand, I have excluded poets now living in Scotland but English or Welsh by birth—I think of Philip Hobsbaum, Robert Nye, Anne Stevenson, Rayne Mackinnon and of Pete Morgan who has returned to England.

There are two poets omitted not by my choice—they said they did not want to be included, and although I do not believe in any form of censorship I have given them their wish.

I have listed only Selected or Collected volumes by Andrew Lang, R. L. Stevenson and John Davidson but otherwise I have listed all the collections of poems I have been able to trace by the other poets included. Some of the poets wrote specialist books in areas of no interest to this bibliography; Sir Ronald Ross, for example, on malaria or Lewis Spence with his many books on mythological subjects. Some, such as John Buchan, wrote on many subjects and, of course, Buchan, like Neil Munro and Stevenson, is better known as a novelist than a poet. I have been unable to trace the birth and death dates of some poets and my placing of these poets is done only by the wildest guesswork.

I compiled the first draft of this bibliography when I began work, in the fifties, on my book *Hugh MacDiarmid and the Scottish Renaissance,* 1964, which has a lengthy bibliography of MacDiarmid and a select bibliography of other poets and of novelists and dramatists up to 1962. At that time I found a bibliographical desert in this field and the situation has not improved much since then. There is, however, the work of Dr. W. R. Aitken on MacDiarmid and I gratefully acknowledge help from his bibliography of Hugh MacDiarmid, the most up-to-date version of which appears in *Hugh MacDiarmid. A Critical Survey* edited by Duncan Glen, 1972. This bibliography could not have been so complete without the active help of lists of their work from most of the living poets who are included in it; I am greatly indebted to all these poets for their generous help. I wish also to thank Mr. J. K. Annand for enthusiastic help in tracing the birth and death dates of some of the poets. I have to thank Mr. Hugh MacDiarmid, or Dr C. M. Grieve, for making time, in an already over-busy life, to write the Preface to this work. I am, as often before, grateful to the staff of the Reading Room of the British Museum (if I may give it its old title) for their ever-willing help. As always I have to thank my wife for the final typescript and for much patience with my continuing preoccupation with Scottish poetry.

D.G.

Penwortham, Preston.
April 1974.

In her Introduction to her collection of the late Sir Ifor Williams' essays, *The Beginnings of Welsh Poetry*, Rachel Bromwich (University of Wales Press, Cardiff, 1972) remarks on the "unprecedented advances in the three years since 1967 in the publication of responsible translations into English from early Welsh poetry, and of the books and articles in English concerning it", and she quotes Sir Ifor himself expressing the wish that he might re-edit each one of his books "since new light breaks in upon us constantly as we struggle forwards" and commenting in a later work on "the immense progress" which Old Welsh studies had achieved during the preceding forty years.

This cumulative progress in a short space of time, with all its correction of the errors of previous writers, is not merely a Welsh phenomenon today but a world-wide one; and it certainly applies very fully to Scottish literature. There has been an ever-accelerating interest in the subject, and a vast outpouring of books, articles, theses and dissertations. This has been called "the Scottish Renaissance" or "the Scottish Literary Revival"; and dates from the early twenties.

A well-known Scottish journalist and literary essayist, the late Mr. William Power, commented scathingly on the fact that up to then (c. 1923) almost all historians of Scottish literature had excluded work in Gaelic though it had a much longer history and confined themselves to work in English and in Scots. This entailed the assumption that Scottish literature had begun only in the reign of Alexander III, and that the Scots were Anglo-Saxons. This was in keeping with the insistence that Scottish literature was merely a sub-division of Eng. Lit., and accorded with the fact that it was not taught in any of our universities, colleges, or schools.

There has been a wonderful change in that in the past decade. There are now courses in Scottish literature in all our universities and students are able to graduate in the subject. Glasgow University, indeed, has now a Department of Scottish Literature. Cheap editions (which suit the purses of students and school pupils) of Scottish Classics have become increasingly available, and alongside these there has been a continuous labour of critical re-assessment without parallel in any previous phase of our literary history.

Inevitably in the long period of English cultural imperialism, literature in Gaelic has suffered far more than literature in Scots; but here too there have been great developments in the past twenty to thirty years, and while the output of books on the subject does not rival that on Welsh literature, the omens here are very favourable indeed. As Professor Derick Thomson (Ruaraidh MacThómais), who holds the Chair of Celtic in

Glasgow University, observes in his splendid *An Introduction to Gaelic Poetry* (Gollancz, 1974), "We are not concerned with prophecy in this account of Gaelic poetry over the centuries, but looking back over the history of that poetry we can scarcely fail to notice how tenacious tradition has been, and yet how innovation is eventually acclimatised within tradition. In the poetry of the last half-century or less we have seen such a process largely accomplished once again, and the possibilities of exploitation of new and new-old styles seem considerable still. The reservoir of talent still seems formidable . . . and we may await the next half-century with lively interest."

This is at least as true of literature in Scots.

In practically any subject of the arts and sciences today the amount of research and advance is so great that specialists find it virtually impossible to keep abreast of the immense outpouring of publications; and so far as minority languages and literatures are concerned, all over the world today millions of people are conscious of having been torn away from their native basis and left rootless in an ever-more-bafflingly complex world. So we find them reviving their native languages, even when these have been long obsolete or even devoid of previous literary use. And at the same time they are turning away from the so-called "great world languages" and seeking to re-create indigenous literatures on their traditional bases.

In these circumstances it is more than ever vital that a "continuous audit" should be maintained and bibliographies are vitally needed. Dame Rebecca West recently commented on the rapidity with which publications pass out of print and another commentator told how of a hundred books he considered essential to the subject with which he was concerned over ninety were not to be found in any of our big libraries.

Mr. Duncan Glen has rendered an inestimable service to Scottish literature by making this bibliography. As poet, essayist, critic, editor and publisher his services have been extensive and invaluable; and the present one in the mere number of the writers with whose work he deals must be a veritable eye-opener to all lacking in an intimate knowledge of the subject. I remember how in one of his essays the late Professor Douglas Young dealt with a number of Scottish poets of whom (though I have devoted myself intensively to the subject for over half-a-century) I had not heard at all. Another friend of mine told me that he intended to survey all the books of Scottish poetry in the Mitchell Library in Glasgow. But, I said, how on earth are you going to do it? For there are over 3,000 of them. "Oh", he replied, airily, "I'll just computerise the lot".

Mr. Glen has been his own computer for many years and has a probably unequalled knowledge of the field. He writes from the inside of the great developments I have mentioned, but, even so, he has had to omit a lot of pamphlets, as also poems collected in book form, and many of the young Gaelic poets with whom Professor Derick Thomson deals are omitted here since they have not yet published in book form or pamphlet form and that is a qualification for entry, while of course it has been quite impossible to list all the people who have appeared in magazines.

Mr. Lewis Mumford (friend and pupil of Professor Patrick Geddes) has well said in *The Myth of the Machine* that: "No modern technological device surpasses in its articulation of its parts or its functional fitness the qualities of the least important language". No good Scot, of course, could agree that either Scottish Gaelic or Lallans is among "the least of these", but the point applies equally to all "little languages" and their literatures, no matter how small a number of people can speak or read them.

The bibliography covers the work of Scottish poets from Andrew Lang born in 1844 (died 1912) to Andrew Greig born over a hundred years later in 1951—quite a span and, of course, it shows dramatically in the work as I will show, but geographically at least Lang and Greig can be quite close together. Lang wrote of St. Andrews and Greig has written of his home town of Anstruther. First Lang, in his poem "Almæ Matres", on St. Andrews in 1862:

> St. Andrews by the northern sea,
> A haunted town it is to me!
> A little city, worn and gray,
> The gray North Ocean girds it round;
> And o'er the rocks, and up the bay,
> The long sea-rollers surge and sound;
> And still the thin and biting spray
> Drives down the melancholy street,
> And still endure, and still decay,
> Towers that the salt winds vainly beat.
> Ghost-like and shadowy they stand
> Dim-mirrored in the wet sea-sand.

Now Greig's "It's Sunday" which appeared in *Seven New Voices* in 1972:

> It's Sunday in Anstruther and God drifts down Shore Street
> in a blue home-knitted pullover, his eyes
> full of ears, and his body not obstructing the light.
> And though his mind is on other things
> (like a quite-new colour, or if the grass weren't green),
>
> He drops into the kirk, to sit as sunlight
> on a rear pew. He joins the congregation in song,
> absent-mindedly blessing everyone there
>   (and as an afterthought, the wide world,
>   because it's Sunday, and everyone's singing,
>   and in the street you smiled at Him).

Yes, God is as close as you to me,
and never slips between. He
returns to thinking about His favourite colours,
Blue and Green, and his alias, Apollo,
while we sit in the clear sunlight of the world's church.

But Lang's poem is also of Oxford 1865 and, unlike Greig's, ends nostalgically and
sentimentally:

> All these hath Oxford: all are dear,
> But dearer far the little town,
> The drifting surf, the wintry year,
> The college of the scarlet gown,
> St. Andrews by the northern sea,
> That is a haunted town to me!

There are, however, poets of this time who are much more nostalgic and sentimental
than Lang. Some, such as Charles Murray (1864-1941), built huge sales of their poetry
on it. The last poem in Murray's much-reprinted *Hamewith* is as good a bad example
as any. "Scotland Our Mother" is its title:

> Scotland our Mither—this from your sons abroad,
> Leavin' tracks on virgin veld that never kent a road,
> Trekkin' on wi' weary feet, an' faces turned fae hame,
> But lovin' aye the auld wife across the seas the same . . .
>
> Scotland our Mither—we've bairns you've never seen—
> Wee things that turn them northward when they kneel down at e'en;
> They plead in childish whispers the Lord on high will be
> A comfort to the auld wife—their granny o'er the sea.

To be fair to Murray he could write much better than that as his "Gin I Was God"
shows:

> Gin I was God, sittin' up there abeen,
> Weariet nae doot noo a' my darg was deen,
> Deaved wi' the harps an' hymns oonendin' ringing',
> Tired o' the flockin' angels hairse wi' singin',
> To some clood-edge I'd daunder furth an', feth,
> Look ower an' watch hoo things were gyaun aneth.
> Syne, gin I saw hoo men I'd made mysel'
> Had startit in to pooshan, sheet and fell,
> To reive an' rape, an' fairly mak' a hell
> O' my braw birlin' Earth—a hale week's wark—
> I'd cast my coat again, rowe up my sark,
> An', or they'd time to lench a second ark,
> Tak' back my word an' sen' anither spate,
> Droon oot the hale hypothec, dicht the sklate,
> Own my mistak', an', aince I'd cleared the brod,
> Start a' thing owre again, gin I was God.

Naturally enough Scottish poets continue to be interested in God, as Andrew Greig's poem has already shown, and another contemporary poet who links with both Murray and Greig in that he now lives in Anstruther (like Greig) and originally came from the North-East (like Murray) is Alastair Mackie (b. 1925). Mackie's "In Absentia" shows the revolution of form and scope which has taken place in poetry in Scots since Murray and, indeed, since MacDiarmid who instigated the first post-Murray revolution.

> "We've no heard frae God this while,"
> said ane o the angels.
> It was at a synod
> o the metaphors.
>
> Cam a wind;
> it was aabody speirin
> "Wha?"
> intill themsels.
>
> It was heard by the sauls
> o Baudelaire and Pascal.
> They fell thro the muckle hole
> opened by the question.
>
> I the boddom Jesus sweatit
> "Consummatum est."
> And Nietzsche
> hou he laucht and laucht.
>
> The maist o the fowk bein neither
> philosophers or theologians
> kept gaun tae the kirk.
> **Whiles, like.**
>
> Syne God said: "Noo I'm awa,
> mak a kirk or a mill o't."
>
> And God gaed tae the back o beyond
> i the midst o aathing.

A better "God" poem than Murray's of the early years of the century is "Mercy o' Gode" by Pittendrigh MacGillivray (1856-1938); it has a movement which makes it more difficult to date than Murray's poem:

> Twa bodachs, I mind, had a threep ae day,
>> Aboot man's chief end—
>> Aboot man's chief end.
> Whan the t'ane lookit sweet his words war sour,
> Whan the tither leuch out his words gied a clour,

> But whilk got the better I wasna sure—
>   I wasna sure,
>   An' needna say.

MacGillivray, however, was not popular like Murray, or like his predecessor James Logie Robertson (1846-1922) whose poems (popularly known as Hughies) were well-known through newspaper publication. They were published under the pen-name of "Hugh Haliburton" and, whilst trying to be fair to Robertson, I can do no better than quote from the depressing "A Wet Day" which is sub-titled "Hughie's Pity for the Tinklers":

> The mist lies like a plaid on plain,
> The dyke-taps a' are black wi' rain,
> A soakit head the clover hings,
> On ilka puddle rise the rings . . .
>
> On sic a day wha taks the gate?
> The tinkler, an' his tousie mate;
> He foremost wi' a nose o' flint,
> She sour an' sulky, yards ahint . . .
>
> They're doun the road, they're oot o' sicht,
> They'll reach the howff by fa' o' nicht,
> In Poussie Nancy's cowp the horn,
> An' tak' the wanderin' gate the morn.

But not all the rural Scots poets were as facile and superficial as Robertson and the two female poets Violet Jacob (1863-1946) and Marion Angus (1866-1946) are still worthy of reading not only in anthologies but in selected volumes such as Mrs. Jacob's *The Scottish Poems of Violet Jacob* published in 1944 and Marion Angus's *Selected Poems* edited by Maurice Lindsay and with a personal memoir by Helen B. Cruickshank in 1950. There is a tendency to group these two poets together but it does now seem that Marion Angus is the finer poet although both will finally be read for only two or three poems each. Marion Angus's "Mary's Song" is a fine lyric and although well-known is worth quoting in full to show what the pre-MacDiarmid Scots poets could achieve:

> I wad ha'e gi'en him my lips tae kiss,
> Had I been his, had I been his;
> Barley breid and elder wine,
> Had I been his as he is mine.
>
> The wanderin' bee it seeks the rose;
> Tae the lochan's bosom the burnie goes;
> They grey bird cries at evenin's fa',
> "My luve, my fair one, come awa'."
>
> My beloved sall ha'e this hert tae break,
> Reid, reid wine and the barley cake,
> A he'rt tae break, and a mou' tae kiss,
> Tho' he be nae mine, as I am his.

If Violet Jacob—with Mary Symon (1863-1938)—is the earliest female poet in my bibliography the youngest is Liz Lochhead (b. 1947) who has had a notable success with her *Memo for Spring* published in 1972. She is also represented in *Seven New Voices* which prints a song rather different from that of Marion Angus and yet just as feminine and as moving in its own way. "Wedding March":

> Could I buy a white dress and hope for good weather?
> Could I take something borrowed? Could we bind us together?
> And while visions of Sugar Plums danced in each head
> Could we lie long content on the bed that we'd made?
>
> No, I've not my own house in order enough
> To ever make you a tidy wife.
> Could I learn to waste not
> And want not?
> Make soup from bones
> Save woolscraps, bake scones
> From sour milk? Would I ask for more
> Than to lunch alone on what's left over from the night before?
>
> Could I soothe our children's nighttime bad dream fear
> With nursery rhymes, and never find my cupboard bare?
> Imagine an old handbag full of photographs
> Once in a blue moon I'd drag them out for laughs—
> Smiling at poses I once carefully arranged,
> In hoots at the hemlines and how we've changed.
>
> We'll try. It still is early days.
> I'll try and mend my sluttish ways.
> We'll give our kitchen a new look
> A lick of paint, a spice rack and a recipe book.
> I'll watch our tangled undies bleaching clean
> In the humdrum of the laundromat machine.
> I'll take my pet dog vacuum on its daily walk through rooms.
>
> And, knowing there is no clean sweep, content myself,
> Keeping busy still with brooms.

So far I have concentrated on the pre-MacDiarmid poets who wrote in Scots but at least these poets had the character to be truly bad when they were bad; the English-writing poets of this time now seem to have a dull nothingness hanging over their poems. John Davidson (1857-1909) still enjoys a certain reputation but he is certainly not devoid of the uninteresting monotony I find in the verse of these poets although he also was interested in God—indeed perhaps in being God:

> Henceforth I shall be God; for consciousness
> is God: I suffer; I am God: this Self,

that all the universe combines to quell,
is greater than the universe; and *I*
am that I am. To think and not be God?—
It cannot be! Lo! I shall spread this news,
and gather to myself a band of Gods—
an army, and go forth against the world,
conquering and to conquer. Snowy steppes
of Muscovy, frost-bound Siberian plains,
and scalding sands of Ethiopia,
where groans oppress the bosom of the wind,
and men in gangs are driven to icy graves,
or lashed to brutish slavery under suns
where sheer beams scorch and flay like burning blades,
shall ring, enfranchised, with divine delight.

And it goes on and on. Not that once-famous lyrics are less boring, such as "The Stirrup Cup" by Douglas Ainslie (1865-1950) which begins:

Lady, whose ancestor
   Fought for Prince Charlie,
Met once and nevermore,
   No time for parley!

Yet drink a glass with me
   "Over the water";
Memories pass to me,
   Chieftain's granddaughter!

"Say, will he come again?"
   Nay, lady, never.
"Say, will he never reign?"
   Yea, lady, ever.

And ends with all the irrelevance of so many modern Jacobite songs:

Back to his native land
   Over the water:
Here's to Prince Charlie and
   Lochiel's granddaughter!

But being backward-looking can take other dead-hand forms, as in "To Olive" by Lord Alfred Douglas (1870-1945) which begins uncomfortably sadly:

When in dim dreams I trace the tangled maze
   Of the old days that held and fashioned me,
   And to the sad assize of Memory
From the wan roads and misty time-trod ways,
The timid ghosts of dead forgotten days
   Gather to hold their piteous colloquy,
   Chiefly my soul bemoans the lack of thee
And those lost seasons empty of thy praise.

And ends even more uncomfortably in the face of death:

> And I, in the dark ante-room of Death,
> Will wait for you with ever-outstretched hands
> And ears strained for your little timid feet;
> And in the listening darkness, when your breath
> Pants in distress, my arms will be like bands
> And all my weakness like your winding-sheet.

Not that the Scots-writing poets of this time were usually any better at avoiding the sentimental when faced by death. Here is "There's Nane o' My Ain to Care" by William Ogilvie (1891-1939):

> There's nane o' my ain to care,
> There's nane to mind me now,
> There's nane o' my ain to comb my hair,
> There's nane to sponge my mou'.
>
> There's nane o' my ain to care,
> Strange han's sall straighten me,
> Strangers sall fauld about my limbs
> The claes o' my deid body.

But at least there have been Scottish poems which can face up to death with the saving grace of humour as, for example, "The Grave-digger" by Roderick Watson Kerr (1895-1960):

> A digger he digs in the dark,
> In the naked remains of a wood,
> For his friend that lies stiff and stark,
> On his head hard blood for a hood:
> The digging is painful and slow,
> Yet the digger he sweats like a slave;
> But he did not know what I now know:
> The digger he dug his own grave.

Watson Kerr was one of the directors of the Porpoise Press which did so much in the twenties to encourage Scottish poets and, indeed, novelists. Almost every Scottish poet of the period seems to have had at least one small pamphlet published by the Press. Others associated with the Press before it was taken over by Faber & Faber were George Malcolm Thomson and John Gould. It was also directed by Charles Graves (b. 1892) who has continued to publish collections of poems down to his *Collected Poems* (1972). He has also edited an anthology, with Alice V. Stuart (b. 1899) whose *The Unquiet Tide* was published in 1971, entitled *Voice and Verse* which is due for publication in 1974.

But to return to humorous poems connected with death the most famous must be "Last Lauch" by Douglas Young (1913-1973) and which looks like being the poem by which Young will be remembered:

The Minister said it wald dee,
   the cypress-buss I plantit.
But the buss grew til a tree,
   naething dauntit.

It's growan, stark and heich,
   derk and straucht and sinister,
kirkyairdielike and dreich.
   But whaur's the Minister?

Mention of William Ogilvie leads naturally to the other Ogilvie, Will H. (1869-1963) and to his "The Blades of Harden" which belongs to a tradition, originating in Walter Scott, that we seem to have outgrown at long last.

Ho! for the blades of Harden!
   Ho! for the driven kye!
The broken gate and the lances' hate,
   And a banner red on the sky!
The rough road runs by the Carter;
   The white foam creams on the rein;
Ho! for the blades of Harden!
   "There will be moonlight again."

On the subject of border verse it is interesting to compare T. S. Cairncross on "Langholm" with what Hugh MacDiarmid was later to make of Langholm. Here is part of Cairncross's effort:

It lies by the heather slopes,
Where God spilt the wine of the moorland
Brimming the beaker of hills. Lone it lies
A rude outpost: challenging stars and dawn,
And down from remoteness
And the Balladland of the Forest
The Pictish Esk trails glory,
Rippling the quiet eaves
With the gold of the sun . . .

The little town shall fold itself to rest
With through its dreams the chequered river gleaming
In luminous peace!

And MacDiarmid on another river of Langholm, "By Wauchopeside":

Thrawn water? Aye, owre thrawn to be aye thrawn!
I ha'e my wagtails like the Wauchope tae,
Birds fu' o' fechtin' spirit, and o' fun,
That whiles jig in the air in lichtsome play
Like glass-ba's on a fountain, syne stand still
Save for a quiver, shoot up an inch or twa, fa' back
Like a swarm o' winter-gnats, or are tost aside,
     By their inclination's kittle loup,
     To balance efter hauf a coup.

There's mair in birds than men ha'e faddomed yet.
Tho' maist churn oot the stock sangs o' their kind
There's aiblins genius here and there; . . .

With MacDiarmid we come, of course, to the greatest poet of my bibliography and to the watershed of Scottish poetry of this century. His early work in English, however, gave little hint of the great poetry that was to come and it sat quite happily with that of such poets as George Reston Malloch (1875-1953) and Robert Crawford (1877-1931) and even older poets like Ronald C. Macfie whose "Lilies" is a fair example of his style:

The solid world of sense dissolves away;
The forest swoons; the mountains swing and sway;
The sea becomes a blue amorphous mist,
Like vapours of a melted amethyst;
The whole round globe is as a bubble blown;
Nothing seems real save your soul alone.
For through your lucent eyes our dazzled sight
Espies the glimmer of immortal light;
And through your eyelid lilies sees enshrined
The deathless lilies of Eternal Mind,
And all things seem unreal and untrue
Beside the bright apocalypse of you.

Linked in my mind with Macfie is his fellow scientist Sir Ronald Ross (1857-1932). Ross was the only Scot to appear in the first volume of *Georgian Poetry* and he fits in well enough as a minor figure in that company and indeed in the company of the Scottish Georgians whom C. M. Grieve gathered together in his *Northern Numbers* (1920-22) anthologies. Ross appeared in the second series of *Northern Numbers* in 1921 with four poems including "Song of the Moon" which begins:

Come all creatures of delight,
Beauty's brightest in the night.
I am Beauty, and I bear
Emeralds in my amber hair,
And a crystal gemmary
To adorn earth, air and sea.
I am watching Wisdom too,
For, while others dream, I do
Light the world to let men know
Where's the way for them to go.
I am Love, for I behold
All things ever and of old; . . .

Also in the second series of *Northern Numbers* was Lewis Spence (1874-1955) with Georgian poems in English but soon Spence was to begin, or had already begun, experimenting with Middle Scots although these poems now seem too much like literary exercises as in the often anthologised, "The Queen's Bath-house, Hoylrood":

Time that has dinged doun castels and hie toures
And cast great crouns like tinsel in the fire,
That halds his hand for palace nor for byre
Stands sweir at this, the oe of Venus' boures.

Not Time himself can dwall withouten floures
Though aiks maun fa' the rose sall bide entire;
So sall this diamant of a queen's desire
Outflourish all the stanes that Time devours.
Mony a strength his turret-heid sall tine
Ere this sall fa' whare a queen lay in wine,
Whose lamp was her ain lily flesh and star.
The walls of luve the mair triumphant are
Gif luve were waesome habiting that place;
Luve has maist years that has a murning face.

With Spence's poem we have definitely moved into the *idea* of a revival of Scots as a full literary language fit to measure up to any subject that is the concern of man, or indeed of woman as among those influenced by the renaissance movement led by MacDiarmid in the twenties was Helen B. Cruickshank (b. 1886) who is the oldest living poet in my bibliography and continues to be a kind friend to many poets. Miss Cruickshank's famous poem "Shy Geordie" continues in the pre-MacDiarmid tradition but her "The Ponnage Pool", with a quote from MacDiarmid at its head, shows her fine awareness of the new more intellectual movement in Scots verse. The poem ends:

I am the deep o' the pule,
The fish, the fisher,
The river in spate,
The broon o' the far peat-moss,
The shingle bricht wi' the flooer
O' the yallow mim'lus,
The martin fleein' across.

I mind o' the Ponnage Pule
On a shinin' mornin',
The saumon fishers
Nettin' the bonny brutes—
I' the slithery dark o' the boddom
O' Charon's Coble
Ae day I'll faddom my doobts.

But in the twenties there were other female Scottish poets, writing in English, who lacked Miss Cruickshank's rootedness in any Scottish tradition. Rachel Annand Taylor (1876-1960) was far removed from Scotland, and any poetic reality, even in her well-known "The Princess of Scotland":

"Who are you that so strangely woke,
    And raised a fine hand?"
Poverty wears a scarlet cloke
    In my land.

"Duchies of dreamland, emerald, rose.
    Lie at your command?"
Poverty like a princess goes
    In my land.

> "Wherefore the mask of silken lace
> Tied with a golden band?"
> *Poverty walks with a wanton grace*
> *In my land.*

Muriel Stuart, a contemporary of Rachel Annand Taylor, is known these days, I imagine, for her poems in Maurice Lindsay's anthology *Modern Scottish Poetry* (second revised edition 1966) but in the twenties she was talked of as the greatest woman poet writing in English and one can understand why as perhaps the only real competition in England was from Edith Sitwell or Rachel Annand Taylor. Writing in *Scottish Scene,* 1934, Lewis Grassic Gibbon saw Miss Stuart as "one of the very few great poets writing in non-experimental English". But Gibbon went on: "Miss Stuart, of Scots origin, has been hailed as a great Scots poet. She is as little Scots as Dante." Of course Gibbon was making a case for his provocative belief that there were only two genuinely *Scottish* literary lights—namely Hugh MacDiarmid and Lewis Spence. Gibbon did, however, go on to suggest that these two poets might be the "precursors of a definite school of Scots literature" and to write of William Soutar (1898-1943): "in William Soutar the Elijah of MacDiarmid may yet have an Elisha."

Soutar wrote a lot of verse which is important for its time and reveals that he had moved a long way out of the depression in which poetry in Scots lay from Burns until MacDiarmid. It has now to be admitted, however, that much of Soutar's poetry is too trifling, and uninteresting, and I am not here referring to his *Seeds in the Wind,* 1933, "poems in Scots for children" which should indeed comprise a "minor classic" as *The Times Literary Supplement* suggested. This is a book which one would expect to be in the hands of huge numbers of Scottish children and yet I suspect that it is out of print. For the general reader Soutar is now, like Violet Jacob and Marion Angus, best approached through a selected volume; in Soutar's case this is *Poems in Scots and English* edited by W. R. Aitken and published in 1961. The Scots poems are vastly superior to those in English. Although the larger volume, *Collected Poems,* published after Soutar's tragically early death and edited by Hugh MacDiarmid, performed a service by printing many previously unpublished poems, it does not show Soutar to best advantage and, indeed, despite its 525 closely filled pages, does not print the poems by which Soutar will be remembered. Poems such as "The Tryst" and, above all, "Song" rightly much-anthologised and well described by Alexander Scott, Soutar's biographer, as standing "supreme among Soutar's lyrics":

> Whaur yon broken brig hings owre;
> Whaur yon water maks nae soun':
> Babylon blaws by in stour:
> Gang doun wi' a sang, gang doun.

> Deep, owre deep, for onie drouth:
> Wan eneuch an ye wud droun:
> Saut, or seelfu', for the mouth;
> Gang doun wi' a sang, gang doun.

Babylon blaws by in stour
Whaur yon water maks nae soun';
Darkness is your only door;
Gang doun wi' a sang, gang doun.

Another poet, ten years younger than Soutar, who has written fine bairn-rhymes is J. K. Annand (b. 1908) but, unlike Soutar, he had to wait a long time for publication in book form. His first collection of bairn-rhymes, *Sing it Aince for Pleisure*, was published in 1965 and since then it has been one of the publishing successes of recent collections of poetry in Scots. A second collection of bairn-rhymes, *Twice for Joy*, followed in 1973 and previously Annand had published a volume of adult poems *Two Voices*, 1968. He has a further collection, *Poems and Translations*, forthcoming.

We can now see that Gibbon could have been more optimistic as MacDiarmid, Spence and Soutar were indeed the forerunners of an ever-growing genuinely Scottish school of poetry, and not only in Scots but also in English and Gaelic. Not that this is a school in the sense that they are alike as sheep; one of the strengths of Scottish poetry since the end of the 1939-45 war has been its diversity. The important poets who have emerged in the forties and fifties are now well identified and some of them have issued, or are about to issue, volumes of *Selected Poems*. They spring to mind and indeed can be found in the anthology *Twelve Modern Scottish Poets*, 1971, edited by Charles King where only Edwin Muir, Hugh MacDiarmid and William Soutar of the poets of the twenties and thirties appear, and this seems a fair critical assessment. The poets represented who emerged in the forties and early fifties are: George Bruce, Robert Garioch, Norman MacCaig, Sydney Goodsir Smith, Tom Scott, Edwin Morgan, Alexander Scott, George Mackay Brown and Iain Crichton Smith. There are others who would challenge for a place in that list, most notably W. S. Graham (b. 1918) and Maurice Lindsay. There is no Gaelic work represented but Sorley Maclean challenges as the equal of any of the poets represented except perhaps MacDiarmid. Also there are younger poets pressing for admission to the established ranks but their time will come yet.

Sydney Goodsir Smith (b. 1915) published *Under the Eildon Tree*—his fifth book of poems—in 1948 and it is a sequence worthy to put beside MacDiarmid's *A Drunk Man Looks at the Thistle*, 1926, which is no small achievement considering that MacDiarmid's masterpiece is perhaps the greatest poem in the whole range of Scottish poetry. Goodsir Smith's masterpiece, although it has gone to a second edition, has never been easy to get and must be best known through excerpts in anthologies, although some of the sections of the poem, such as Elegy XIII, are considered unsuitable for anthologies aimed at the school market and one sometimes gets the impression that all anthologies, almost, are aimed at that market.

> Haill tenements, wards and burghs, counties,
>   Regalities and jurisdictions,
>   Continents and empires
>   Gien owre entire
> Til the joukerie-poukerie!
> Hech, sirs, whatna feck of fockerie!
> Shades o Knox, the hochmagandie!
>   My bonie Edinburrie,

> Auld Skulduggerie!
> Flat on her back sevin nichts o the week,
> Earnin her breid wi her hurdies' sweit.

Goodsir Smith has also written, in more sober mood suitable for a televised poem, of Edinburgh in *Kynd Kittock's Land* and in it he writes appropriately to something my bibliography, in gathering together so many poets, truly shows:

> "We hae forgot muckle, Clarinda,
> Gane wi the rift o' the wind"—
> But ithers rise to tak their places brawlie:
> Grieve and Garioch aye tuim their pints,
> Mackie wheezes, Scott aye propheseezes
> Frae his lofty riggin tree
> While lean MacCaig stauns snuffin the Western seas
> And Brown leads wi his Viking chin
> And winna be rebukit.

These, presumably, are poets to be found in Edinburgh at a certain time and so, presumably again, Mackie is A. D. Mackie (b. 1904) who was revealed to be one of the first to be influenced by MacDiarmid's *A Drunk Man Looks at the Thistle* when his *Poems in Two Tongues* was published in 1928. Scott, one guesses, is Tom Scott (b. 1918) of Edinburgh and not Alexander Scott (b. 1920) who is now of Glasgow although originally of Aberdeen as his magnificent long poem "Heart of Stone" shows:

> The tapmaist ferlie aye the toun itsel,
> Graithed intil granite, stanced in stalliard stane,
> A hard hauld, a sterk steid,
> A breem bield o steive biggins,
> Riven frae raw rock, and rockie-rooted,
> She bares her brou til the bite o the brashy gale
> Or stares back straucht at the skimmeran scaud o the sun,
> Fowr-square til aa the elements, fine or foul,
> Heedless o rain and reek
> (Sen rain can only wash the reek awa),
> For nocht can fyle her adamant face,
> Itsel an armour proof til ilka onding.

Alexander Scott, with his wide interests in and out of Scotland pushed right into his poetry, shows how far poetry in Scots has progressed even since MacDiarmid. His planned *Selected Poems 1943-1973* should be a major publishing event.

Although Tom Scott has lived in Edinburgh for many years and was born in Glasgow he may well be remembered for a sequence of poems on St. Andrews. A St. Andrews far removed from that of Andrew Lang as a short passage from "Auld Sanct-Aundrians —Brand the Builder" can show:

> The supper owre, Brands redds up for the nicht.
> Aiblins there's a schedule for to price,
> Or something nice
> On at the picters—sacont hoose—
> Or some poleetical meetin wants his licht,
> Or aiblins, wi him t-total aa his life,

No able to seek the pub to flee the wife
Daunders out the West Sands "on the loose."
Whatever tis,
The waater slorps frae his elbucks as he synds his phiz.

And this is aa the life he kens there is.

These St. Andrews poems are as yet uncollected and it is at present difficult to see Tom Scott's work as a whole. A much-needed volume, *Musins and Murgeonins,* is planned, however, from Caithness Books which is an enterprising small press owned by John Humphries and directed on the literary side by the poet David Morrison (b. 1941) who has published a whole series of his own collections of poems, mostly in Scots, under his private Scotia imprint.

Although Norman MacCaig (b. 1910) has lived all his life in Edinburgh he has written important poetry influenced, as Goodsir Smith said in his poem, by the Western Highlands but the metaphysics of MacCaig are perhaps what make him the most important English-writing Scottish poet of this century—which is the equivalent of saying of all time. As he says in the memorable ending to the first poem in his *Selected Poems,* 1971:

Self under self, a pile of selves I stand
Threaded on time, and with metaphysic hand
Lift the farm like a lid and see
Farm within farm, and in the centre, me.

Robert Garioch (b. 1909) is well established as a poet of Edinburgh and it is now often forgotten that he spent years in England but his "Edinburgh Sonnets", printed in his important *Selected Poems,* have linked him irreplaceably with the capital city which he delights in bringing down a peg as in "Did Ye See Me?" with its heavy ironic rhymes:

I'll tell ye of ane great occasioun:
I tuke pairt in a graund receptioun.
Ye cannae hae the least perceptioun
hou pleased I was to get the invitatioun

tae assist at ane dedicatioun.
And richtlie sae; frae its inceptioun
the hale ploy was my ain conceptioun;
I was asked to gie a dissertatioun.

The functioun was held in the aipen air,
a peety, that; the keelies of the toun,
a toozie lot, gat word of the affair.

We cudnae stop it: they jist gaithert roun
to mak sarcastic cracks and grin and stare.
I wisht I hadnae worn my M.A. goun.

Another Edinburgh poet, too young to be mentioned in Smith's poem, is Donald Campbell (b. 1940) who has shown, like Garioch, the vigour of a literary language based on contemporary Edinburgh Scots. He says something important to Scots poets in "Ye Say 'Glass'":

> Ye say "glass"—an I ken whit ye mean
> I think "gless"—but whit are you thinkan?
> A lang strang table lies atween
> the "glass" an the "gless" but naebody's drinkan!
>   We're suppan thegither but missan the taste
>   *for ae single letter is double-glazed*
> I say "gless"—dae ye ken whit I mean?

George Mackay Brown (b. 1921), although in Goodsir Smith's poem, lived in Edinburgh only as a mature student and he soon returned to his native Orkney in which his poetry, and prose, is firmly and most satisfactorily rooted in a real world of "The Poet":

> Therefore he no more troubled the pool of silence
> But put on mask and cloak,
> Strung a guitar
> And moved among the folk.
> Dancing they cried,
> "Ah, how our sober islands
> Are gay again, since this blind lyrical tramp
> Invaded the Fair!"
>
> Under the last dead lamp
> When all the dancers and masks had gone inside
> His cold stare
> Returned to its true task, interrogation of silence.

Edwin Muir (1887-1959) is another poet who was born in Orkney, but he had not the rootedness that Brown enjoys as he soon left the islands for a depressing time in Glasgow and after that he became a wanderer around Europe. He did return to St. Andrews in 1935 and G. S. Fraser (b. 1915) was to write in his poem "Meditation of a Patriot":

> St. Andrews soothes that critic at her breast
> Whose polished verse ne'er gave his soul release.

St. Andrews, to judge from Willa Muir's *Belonging*, 1968, did not soothe Muir but rather led to what Mrs. Muir described as "the uncharacteristic acerbity of Edwin's remarks about Scotland" in *Scott and Scotland*, 1936, and although Fraser would seem to be right in suggesting that Muir's poems did not give him release perhaps the writing of those on Scotland may at least have partially soothed him after the slights and repressions of class-conscious, provincial St. Andrews. To me, however, these Scottish poems are not Muir's best; I prefer those in which he has "One Foot in Eden" or in the horrors of post-war Europe even if they did not give the poet release. In particular I think of "The Horses" where he achieved major poetry. It really needs quoting in full but it does set its quiet but all-pervading horror, yet hope, right from the beginning:

> Barely a twelvemonth after
> The seven days war that put the world to sleep,
> Late in the evening the strange horses came.
> By then we had made our covenant with silence,
> But in the first few days it was so still
> We listened to our breathing and were afraid.

Other poets still writing have been attracted to Orkney, and to Shetland. Charles Senior (b. 1918) lives in Orkney at present and Alastair Mackie lived there for a time and some of his English poems in *Soundings*, 1966, reflect Orkney scenes and life. Another poet who has written Orkney poems—and influential poems they have been— is Ian Hamilton Finlay (b. 1925). They are to be found in his collection *The Dancers Inherit the Party* which was first published by Migrant Press in 1960. The poems in *The Dancers* are notable achievements but these days Finlay is internationally known as the most important British concrete poet. He has been able to maintain his high visual standards through publishing a lot of his work through his own press—the Wild Hawthorn Press—and by working very closely with artists and printers to whom he gives the most detailed instructions. An exhibition of Finlay's work is very impressive but the full effect can often be appreciated only by handling the works and by turning the pages of his books. Not that he is limited to books, having published many cards and folding cards, poem/prints and other poems difficult to define. Finlay has also created works for erection in public places such as sundials in Biggar, Kelso, University of Kent, Canterbury and the neon mural poem at the State Museum, Lodz, Poland. His "Cythera" (extended poem in ceramic and concrete) is being built in the Royal Botanic Gardens, Edinburgh.

James Rankin (b. 1939) whose *Poems*, 1969, was published in the first group of Parklands Poets, which appear under the Akros imprint, has lived in Shetland as his poetry shows. "Back from Jarlshof":

> Walking home from Broo the fish
> Dangling from our hands we saw the
> Houses huddle at the cheek of the voe.
> Vlamnick did the sky; overdone, blue
> Black, thick pigments that reached to
> Norway and back.

The younger poet, Robin Munro (b. 1946) has also written of Jarlshof in his *Shetland, Like the World*, 1973, which is an impressive first collection.

> At Jarlshof
> we went on our knees
> crouching into warrens of the past.
>
> A very little air
> but this was ground built once, and safe.
> I would not be against going back.

At Sumburgh
she has us fastened
in out seats, no change of mind.

The land lets go, and falls down, bouncing.
"A little turbulence."

God's view of standing stones
is very small.

One of the common faults of the pre-MacDiarmid poets of this century was that
their view of the world was very small indeed and allied to this was the fact that often
they sang, as has been said before, of a day, and a way of life that was dead. Here are
the Highlands of Neil Munro (1864-1930) and the past as seen through a Celtic Twilight
could not be more falsely in evidence:

Gone in the mist the brave Macleods of Raasay!
Far furth from fortune, sundered from their lands;
And now the last grey stone of Castle Raasay
Lies desolate and levelled with the sands;
But pluck the old isle from its roots deep planted
Where tides cry coronach round the Hebrides,
And it will bleed of the Macleods lamented,
Their loves and memories!

Today the Highlands have authentic voices in the Gaelic poets Sorley Maclean (b.
1911), George Campbell Hay (b. 1915), Derick Thomson (b. 1922), Iain Crichton Smith
(b. 1928) and Donald Macauley (b. 1930) although, of course, Smith is also an established
poet in English—see his *Selected Poems*, 1970—and Hay has been versatile in many
languages as his collection *Wind on Loch Fyne*, 1948, reveals. Recently Iain Crichton
Smith has performed the important service of making Sorley Maclean available in
English translation, and noble translations they are as the following shows:

Now that the ivory towers are down
and my desire is but a thin
shade of a tale that's dead and gone,
there is only: Let me strengthen
my own spirit against pain.

For I have watched while Spain, struck dead,
salted the eyes within my head
and slowed my wheels of pride and blood,
with thoughts of nothingness and death
and heroes who have lost their breath.

And now we see on every side
heart-break and the death of pride,
the nothingness that will deride
every generous thought we nursed
to satisfy the spirit's thirst.

But Smith was not the first poet to translate Maclean and I have long had in my
memory Maclean's "Calbharaigh" in the translation by Douglas Young:

> My een are nae on Calvary
> or the Bethlehem they praise,
> but on shitten back-lands in Glesga toun
> whaur growan life decays,
> and a stairheid room in an Embro land,
> a chalmer o puirtith and skaith,
> whaur monie a shilpet bairnikie
> gaes smoorit doun til daith.

A poet who did have his eyes on a Calvary, at least at the start of the first world war,
was F. V. Branford (1892-1941) and after the powerful restraint of Maclean, even in
translation, his poem appears as a piece of posturing about war or anti-war.

> We thought to find a cross like Calvary's,
> And queened proud England with a diadem
> Of thorns. Impetuous armies clamouring
> For war, from the far utterance of the seas
> We sprang to win a new Jerusalem.
> Now is our shame, for we have seen you fling
> Full-sounding honour from your lips like phlegm
> And bargain up our souls in felonies.

But Branford's use of language and sentiments are perhaps to be preferred to those of
John Buchan (1875-1940) who expressed a Scots kailyard war, or post-war, in "Home-
Thoughts from Abroad". In the poem a soldier thinks of the days after the war and I
will avoid the worst by not quoting the end but only a small extract from the middle:

> I'll haste me back wi' an eident fit
> And settle again in the same auld bit.
> And oh! the comfort to snowk again
> The reek o' my mither's but-and-ben,
> The wee box-bed and the ingle neuk
> And the kail-pat hung frae the chimley-heuk!

Which takes us back to the sentimental post-Burnsian nostalgie that I started with;
Buchan was almost always a literary escapist in his poetry, as in his prose, although like
Charles Murray he did show an interest in giving Scots a new dignity through translation.
But the first notable translator into Scots is neither Buchan nor Murray but Sir Alexander
Gray (1882-1968) whom Buchan included in his pioneering anthology *The Northern
Muse,* 1924. Here is Gray's translation from Heine: "The Kings from the East":

> There were three kings cam frae the East;
> They spiered in ilka clachan:
> "O, which is the wey to Bethlehem,
> My bairns, sae bonnily lachin'?"
>
> O neither young nor auld could tell;
> They trailed till their feet were weary.
> They followed a bonny gowden starn,
> That shone in the lift sae cheery.

> The starn stude ower the ale-hoose byre
> Whaur the stable gear was hingin';
> The owsen mooed, the bairnie grat,
> The kings begoud their singin'.

Since Gray many fine poets have continued the work of translation into Scots including Hugh MacDiarmid, Sydney Goodsir Smith, Tom Scott, Robert Garioch, J. K. Annand, Douglas Young, Alastair Mackie and Edwin Morgan (b. 1920). Most of the translations are difficult to come by but Edwin Morgan has the distinction of having a whole volume, *Wi the Haill Voice,* 1972, devoted to the work of Vladimir Mayakovsky. It is a major piece of translation. Morgan has also been very productive as a translator of many European poets into English, as has Robin Fulton (b. 1937). Both Morgan and Fulton are, of course, also poets in their own right and Morgan has shown a wide range in modern forms including concrete poetry. He is perhaps at his very best when writing of his native Glasgow as in the first of his *Glasgow Sonnets,* 1972:

> A mean wind wanders through the backcourt trash.
> Hackles on puddles rise, old mattresses
> puff briefly and subside. Play-fortresses
> of brick and bric-a-brac spill out some ash.
> Four storeys have no windows left to smash,
> but in the fifth a chipped sill buttresses
> mother and daughter the last mistresses
> of that black block condemned to stand, not crash.
> Around them the cracks deepen, the rats crawl.
> The kettle whimpers on a crazy hob.
> Roses of mould grow from ceiling to wall.
> The man lies late since he has lost his job,
> smokes on one elbow, letting his coughs fall
> thinly into an air too poor to rob.

The change which has taken place in Scottish poetry since the end of the 1939-45 war is seen clearly by comparing the backward-lookingness of William Jeffrey (1896-1946)—who like Morgan worked in Glasgow—with the progressive outlook of Morgan. Also, the new directness of attack in the poetry is well illustrated by a comparison of these two poets. Alexander Scott, who edited Jeffrey's *Selected Poems,* 1951, is no doubt right in pointing to Jeffrey's later work, particularly his dramatic lyrics "The Galleys" and "On Glaister's Hill" as his most important poems in a large output but in his comment on Jeffrey in *The MacDiarmid Makars 1923-1972,* 1972, Scott rightly points to the fact that Jeffrey looked to the past for subjects and so perhaps had doubts "as to the medium's suitability for contemporary themes." My own reaction to Jeffrey's poetry is that he tended to the artificially "poetic" of the literary past rather than to "real" poetic subjects of the present. An example of this is to be seen in his *Fantasia Written in an Industrial Town,* 1933:

> High-stationed o'er the town our windows take
> The amplitude of heaven in their view:
> Pale buds of matin lilies eastwards break,
> And southward, saddled over flanks of blue

And riding cold, remote, majestic, still,
    His belted stars scarce flickering on air,
We see Orion. Do we know his will,
    Or what enthralls him in the zero there?

Another poet of the West of Scotland, and indeed of Glasgow, although he has written of most parts of Scotland, is Maurice Lindsay (b. 1918) who, in 1973, published his *Selected Poems 1942-1972* and it is an accomplished body of work, in Scots and English, that Lindsay has been able to select from his many books of poems.

Recently there has been a stimulating upsurge of younger poets writing with a new sensibility but with their roots set firmly in Glasgow. The most obviously Glasgow of them, in that he sometimes writes in the Glasgow dialect, is Tom Leonard (b. 1944) and his "The Good Thief" is already too well known to need quoting here. For those who have not encountered it, it can be found in his *Poems, 1973.*

But this poetry of the new nominalist sensibility has not been confined to Glasgow poets. In Edinburgh Alan Jackson (b. 1938) has been writing with an unpolite modern sensibility as in " 'tiny nippled men' ":

> tiny nippled men wander through the auld toon
> in delicate high voices they cry
> "we are what you're coming to"
>
> "get away fae me, ye daft poofs"
> the big drunk labourer shouts
> and falls down the steps into the bog in the grassmarket

Jackson does not like national labels but despite this he is too good a poet to avoid being true, through his use of language, to his Scottishness in his poetry. David Black's (b. 1941) language is less obviously Scottish but he has been exploring new rich areas through a very literary imagination for all the newness of his forms. I suspect Andrew Lang would have been shocked or at least disturbed by Black's use of St. Andrews in "St. Andrews: Thoughts on Mutation":

> new goals of reproduction
> men got for a knack with ciphers
> a more agitated cortex
> an endurance in capsules)
>
> rain   rain falling
>
> I stare out through a watery window
> lupins in fawn and flame
>
> (. . . that it should be my dear Darwin
> ancestor of these filthinesses

But perhaps Lang would have been able to accept the St. Andrews of George Bruce

(b. 1909) more easily although Bruce deals with ideas well beyond Lang's reach in poetry
in "A Gateway to the Sea (1)":

> Pause stranger at the porch: nothing beyond
> This framing arch of stone, but scattered rocks
> And sea and these on the low beach
> Original to the cataclysm and the dark.

But as Bruce said at the beginning of another St. Andrews poem, "St. Andrews, June,
1946":

> Old tales, old customs and old men's dreams
> Obscure this town. Memories abound.
> In the mild misted air, and in the sharp air
> Toga and gown walk the pier.
> The past sleeps in the stones.

Or Lang in his "St. Andrews Bay at Night":

> When all is done, when all the tale is told,
> And the grey sea-wave echoes as of old.

And Bruce ends "A Gateway to the Sea (1)", a very different poem from any of
Lang's, also at night:

> Under the touch the guardian stone remains
> Holding memory, reproving desire, securing hope
> In the stop of water, in the lull of night
> Before dawn kindles a new day.

Bruce has also written some very fine poems rooted in the Fraserburgh of his youth,
but with new form, including the magnificent "Inheritance" which begins:

> This which I write now
> Was written years ago
> Before my birth
> In the features of my father.

> It was stamped
> In the rock formations
> West of my hometown.
> Not I write,

> But, perhaps William Bruce,
> Cooper.
> Perhaps here his hand
> Well articled in his trade.

George Bruce's *Collected Poems,* 1970, is another good illustration of the transformation that has come over Scottish poetry since the twenties.

But of course the new forms have not been confined to poets writing in English.

I have myself written a Scots which attempts to break new areas of form and sensibility using a Scots language. I like to think that within this "newness" I have shown that even Burns need not be a bad inspiration for a poem:

> This is a gey ugly monument to you
> Robert Burns 1759-
> 1796.
>
> Is that no final. And yet there is
> you and I Robert Burns. There's nae easy
> beginnin or end. Nae settin apairt o thae twa.
> There's the moment we live by
> as we dee.
>
> The registrar o births and daiths
> (and mairriages) nae dout he would see me
> gaein furrit step by step to that second
> date. And yet we traivel backwards
> —as much as furrit onyweys. You ken that
> in that mool.
>
> We hae moments o peace we say
> and deep sleeps. We hae our moments
> and dee
> as we live. That's aa the time there is
> Robert Burns. Robert Burns
> 1759-1796.

To Andrew Lang and R. L. Stevenson (1850-94) it would no doubt come as a great surprise that there has been this optimistic revival of Scots into new modern forms of expression and into a poetry that recognises no limitation of scope. Stevenson wrote pessimistically in his "The Makar to Posterity":

> "No' bein' fit to write in Greek,
>   I wrote in Lallan,
> Dear to my heart as the peat-reek,
>   Auld as Tantallon.
>
> "Few spak it then, an' noo there's nane.
> My puir auld sangs lie a' their lane,

But far from standing a' their lane Stevenson's songs are now seen as small things at the beginning of the major Scottish poetic revival which has taken place during this century and which the generations of poets in my bibliography have all contributed to in some way.

LANG, Andrew (1844-1912)
Poetry: The Poetical Works, ed. Mrs Lang, 4 vols (1923).

ROBERTSON, James Logie ("Hugh Haliburton") (1846-1922)
Poetry: Horace in Homespun (1886, see also Memorial Volume
1925); Ochil Idylls (1891). *Prose:* "For Puir Auld
Scotland's Sake" (1887); In Scottish Fields (1890);
Furth in Field (1894).

STEVENSON, Robert Louis (1850-94)
Poetry: Collected Poems, ed. Janet Adam Smith (1950).

HENDRY, Hamish (1855-   )
Poetry: Burns from Heaven (1897); Red Apple and Silver
Bells (1897); A Scots Dominie (1924); Children's Verse
of Town and Country (1926); Poems: English and Scottish
(1926).

DOUGLAS, Sir George (1856-1935)
Poetry: Poems of a Country Gentleman (1897); Poems of
the Open Air (1927); Gleanings in Prose and Verse,
ed. Oliver Hilson (1938). *Edited:* Contemporary Scottish
Verse (1893); Book of Scottish Poetry (1911).

MACGILLIVRAY, James Pittendrigh (1856-1938)
Poetry: Pro Patria (1915); Bog-myrtle and Peat Reek (1922).

DAVIDSON, John (1857-1909)
Poetry: Poems by John Davidson, ed. R.M. Wenley (1924);
Poems and Ballads, ed. R.D. Macleod (1959); John
Davidson: A Selection of his Poems, ed. Maurice Lindsay
(1961); The Poems of John Davidson, ed. Andrew Turnbull,
2 vols (1973).

ROSS, Sir Ronald (1857-1932)
Poetry: Philosophies (1910); Psychologies (1919);
Poems (1928).

ANDERSON, Jessie Annie (1861-   )
Poetry: Songs in Season (1901); Songs of Hope and
Courage (1902); Lyrics of Life and Love (1903);
Old-World Sorrow (1903); Lyrics of Childhood (1905);
A Book of the Wonder Ways (1907); Breaths from Four
Winds (1911); This is Nonsense (1926); A Singer's
Year (1928).

JACOB, Violet (1863-1946)
Poetry: Verses (1905); Songs of Angus (1915);
More Songs of Angus (1918); Bonnie Joann (1921);
Two New Poems (1924); The Northern Lights (1927);
The Scottish Poems of Violet Jacob (1944).

SYMON, Mary (1863-1938)
Poetry: Deveron Days (1933).

MUNRO, Neil (1864-1930)
Poetry: The Poetry of Neil Munro (1931).

MURRAY, Charles (1864-1941)
Poetry: Hamewith (1900 and enlarged 1909); A Sough
o' War (1917); In the Country Places (1920).

WINGATE, Walter (1865-1918)
Poetry: Poems (1919).

AINSLIE, Douglas (1865-1950)
Poetry: Escarlamonde (1893); John of Damascus (1901);
Moments (1905); The Song of the Stewarts (1909); Mirage
(1911); Chosen Poems (1926); Pleasure (1938).

ANGUS, Marion (1866-1946)
Poetry: The Lilt (1922); The Tinker's Road (1924); Sun and
Candlelight (1927); The Singin' Lass (1929); The Turn of
the Day (1931); Lost Country (1937); Selected Poems, ed.
Maurice Lindsay and a Personal Memoir by Helen B.
Cruickshank (1950).

MACFIE, Ronald C. (1867-1931)
Poetry: Granite Dust (1892); New Poems (1904); War (1918);
Odes (1919); Collected Poems (1929); The Last Poems (1933);
The Love Poems (1934); The Complete Poems (1937).

OGILVIE, W.H. (1869-1963)
Poetry: Hearts of Gold (1903); Fair Girls and Gray Horses
(1906); Rainbows and Witches (1907); Whaup o' the Rede
(1909); The Land we Love (1910); The Overlander (1913);
Verses (1922); Scattered Scarlet (1923); A Handful of
Leather (1928); The Collected Sporting Verse (1932);
Saddles Again (1937); From Sunset to Dawn (1946).

DOUGLAS, Lord Alfred (1870-1945)
Poetry: Poems (1896); The City of the Soul (1899); Collected
Poems (1919); In Excelsis (1924); The Duke of Berwick (1925);
Nine Poems (1926); [Selected Poems] (1926); The Complete
Poems (1928); Lyrics (1935). *Prose:* The Autobiography (1929).

CAIRNCROSS, T.S. (1872-   )
Poetry: The Return of the Master (1905); From the Kilpatrick
Hills (1921); The Scot at Hame (1922).

SPENCE, Lewis (1874-1955)
Poetry: Songs Satanic and Celestial (1913); The Phoenix (1923);
Plumes of Time (1926); Weirds and Vanities (1927); Collected
Poems (1953).

BUCHAN, John (1st Lord Tweedsmuir) (1875-1940)
Poetry: Poems, Scots and English (1917).
Prose: Montrose (1928); Sir Walter Scott (1932).
Edited: The Northern Muse (1924).

MALLOCH, George Reston (1875-1953)
Poetry: Lyrics and other poems (1913); Poems and
Lyrics (1916); Poems (1920); Human Voices (1930); The
Moment's Monuments (1932). *Plays:* Arabella (1912);
Thomas the Rhymer (1924); Soutarness Water (1927);
The Grenadier (1930); Down in the Forest (1935).

TAYLOR, Rachel Annand (1876-1960)
Poetry: Poems (1904); Rose and Vine (1909); The Hours
of Fiammetta (1910); The End of Fiammetta (1923).
Prose: Aspects of the Italian Renaissance (1923);
Leonardo the Florentine (1927); Dunbar: the Poet and
his Period (1931).

CRAWFORD, Robert (1877-1931)
Poetry: Poems (1924); A Ballad (1925); In Quiet Fields
(1929).

LEE, Joseph (1878-1949)
Poetry: Poems. Tales of our Town (1910); Ballads of
Battle (1916); Work-a-day Warriors (1917).

HORNE, J.G.
Poetry: A Lan'wart Loon (1928); Flooer o' the Ling (1936).

FERGUSON, John (1879-1928)
Poetry: Thyrea (1912, see also fifteenth (memorial)
edition with additional sonnets, 1929).

STUART, Muriel
Poetry: Christ at Carnival (1916); The Cockpit of Idols
(1918); Poems (1922); Selected Poems (1927);
Gardener's Nightcap (1938).

BOYLE, Mary E. (1881-   )
Poetry: Pilate in Exile at Vienne (1915); Aftermath (1916);
Daisies and Apple Trees (1922); Herodias Inconsolable (1923).

SACKVILLE, Lady Margaret (1881-1963)
Poetry: Poems (1901); A Hymn to Dionysus (1905); Bertud
(1911); Lyrics (1912); Songs of Aphrodite (1913); The Pageant
of War (1916); Selected Poems (1919); Epitaphs (1921);
Poems (1923); A Rhymed Sequence (1924); Romantic Ballads
(1926); Twelve Little Poems (1931); Ariadne by the Sea
(1932); Collected Poems (1939); Return to Song (1943); The
Lyrical Woodlands (1945); Miniatures (1947); Tree Music
(1947).

COCKER, W.D. (1882-1970)
Poetry: The Dreamer (1920); Dandie (1925); The Bubbly-jock
(1929); Poems, Scots and English (1932); Further Poems
(1935); New Poems (1949).

GRAY, Sir Alexander (1882-1968)
Poetry: Songs and Ballads, chiefly from Heine (1920);
Any Man's Life (1924); Poems (1925); Songs from Heine (1928);
Gossip (1928); Arrows (1932); Selected Poems, ed. Maurice
Lindsay (1948); Sir Halewyn (1949); Four-and-forty (1954);
Historical Ballads of Denmark (1958).

ROBERTSON, Edith Anne (1883-1973)
Poetry: Voices frae the City o Trees (1955); Collected
Ballads and Poems in the Scots Tongue (1967); Translations
into the Scots Tongue of Poems by Gerard Manley Hopkins
(1968); Forest Voices (1969).

YOUNG, Andrew (1885-1971)
Poetry: Boaz and Ruth (1920); The Death of Eli (1921);
Thirty-One Poems (1922); The Bird-Cage (1926); The Cuckoo
Clock (1928); Winter Harvest (1933); The White Blackbird
(1935); Collected Poems (1936); The Green Man (1947);
Collected Poems (1950); Into Hades (1952); Quiet as Moss
(1959); Complete Poems, arranged and introduced by Leonard
Clark (1974).

CRUICKSHANK, Helen B. (1886)
Poetry: Up the Noran Water (1934); Sea Buckthorn (1954);
The Ponnage Pool (1968); Collected Poems (1971).
Edited: Selected Poems of Marion Angus (with Maurice
Lindsay) (1950).

HAMILTON, W.H. (1886-1958)
Poetry: Gauldry (1920); The Desire of the Moth (1925).
Edited: Holyrood. A Garland of Modern Scots Poems (1929).

MUIR, Edwin (1887-1959)
Poetry: First Poems (1925); Chorus of the Newly Read
(1926); Six Poems (1932); Variations on a Time Theme
(1934); Journeys and Places (1937); The Narrow Place
(1943); The Voyage (1946); The Labyrinth (1949);
Collected Poems 1921-1951, ed. J.C. Hall (1952);
Prometheus (1954); One Foot in Eden (1956); Collected
Poems 1921-1958 (1960); Selected Poems, ed. T.S. Eliot
(1965). *Prose:* Latitudes (1924); Transition (1926);
The Marionette (novel) (1927); The Structure of the Novel
(1928); John Knox (1929); The Three Brothers (novel)
(1931); Poor Tom (novel) (1932); Scottish Journey (1935);
Scott and Scotland (1936); Social Credit and the Labour
Party. An Appeal (1937); The Present Age from 1914
(1939); The Story and the Fable (1940); The Scots and
Their Country (1946); Essays on Literature and Society
(1949); An Autobiography (1954); The Estate of Poetry
(1962). *Edited:* New Poets 1959 (Iain Crichton Smith,
Karen Gershon and Christopher Levenson) (1959).

MACARTHUR, Bessie J.B. (1889)
Poetry: The Starry Venture (1934); Scots Poems (1938);
Last Leave (1943); From Daer Water (1962); And Time
Moves On (1972). *Play:* The Clan of Lochlann (1927).

OGILVIE, William (1891-1939)
Poetry: The Witch (1923); My Mither's Aunt (1926).

BRANFORD, F.V. (1892-1941)
Poetry: Titans and Gods (1922); Five Poems (1922);
The White Stallion (1924).

GRAVES, Charles (1892)
Poetry: Selected Poems of Pierre de Ronsard (translated)
(1924); The Bamboo Grove (1925); The Wood of Time (1938);
Votive Sonnets (1965); Lyrics of Pierre de Ronsard
(translated) (1967); Emblems of Love and War (1970);
Collected Poems (1972). *Edited:* Voice and Verse (with
Alice V. Stuart) (forthcoming 1974).

"MACDIARMID, Hugh" (C.M. Grieve) (1892)
Poetry: Sangschaw (1925); Penny Wheep (1926); A Drunk Man
Looks at the Thistle (1926, 2nd edition 1953, 3rd edition
1956, 4th edition 1962, 5th edition 1969, 6th edition
(ed. John C. Weston) 1971); The Lucky Bag (1927); To
Circumjack Cencrastus (1930); O Wha's Been Here Afore Me,
Lass (1931); First Hymn to Lenin (1931); Tarras (1932);
Scots Unbound (1932); Second Hymn to Lenin (1932); Stony
Limits (1934); Selected Poems (1934); The Birlinn of
Clanranald by Alexander MacDonald (translated) (1935);
Second Hymn to Lenin and other poems (1935); Direadh (1938);
Speaking for Scotland, ed. Paul Potts (1939); Cornish
Heroic Song for Valda Trevlyn (1943); Selected Poems, ed.
R. Crombie Saunders (1944); Speaking for Scotland. Selected
Poems (1946); Poems of the East-West Synthesis (1946);
A Kist of Whistles (1947); Selected Poems, ed. Oliver Brown
(1954, 2nd edition 1955); In Memoriam James Joyce (1955, 2nd
edition 1956); Stony Limits and Scots Unbound (1956); The
Battle Continues (1957); Three Hymns to Lenin (1957); The
Kind of Poetry I Want (1961); Bracken Hills in Autumn (1962);
Collected Poems (1962, revised edition 1967); Poetry Like
the Hawthorn (1962); The Blaward and the Skelly (1962); An
Apprentice Angel (1963); Poems to Paintings by William
Johnstone 1933 (1963); Harry Martinson. Aniara (translated
with Elspeth Harley Schubert) (1963); Two Poems (1964);
The Ministry of Water (1964); Six Vituperative Verses, ed.
Duncan Glen (1964); Poet at Play, ed. Duncan Glen (1965);
The Fire of the Spirit (1965); The Burning Passion (1965);
Whuchulls (1966); On a Raised Beach (1967, a German trans-
lation by Arno Reinfrank appeared later); The Eemis Stane
(1967); A Lap of Honour (1967); Early Lyrics, ed. J.K. Annand
(1968, 2nd edition 1969); A Clyack-Sheaf (1969); More
Collected Poems (1970); Selected Poems, ed. David Craig and
John Manson (1970); The Hugh MacDiarmid Anthology, ed.
Michael Grieve and Alexander Scott (1972); Song of the
Seraphim (1973). There is a MidNag Poster Poem (No.21) of
MacDiarmid's poem "The Bonnie Broukit Bairn" with graphics

by Birtley Aris. *Prose:* Annals of the Five Senses (also
poetry) (1923, 2nd edition 1930); Contemporary Scottish
Studies (1926); Albyn, or Scotland and the Future (1927);
The Present Position of Scottish Music (1927); The Present
Condition of Scottish Arts and Affairs (1928); The
Scottish National Association of April Fools (1928);
Scotland in 1980 (1929); The Handmaid of the Lord by Ramon
Maria de Tenreiro (translated) (1930); Five Bits of
Miller (1934); Scottish Scene, or The Intelligent Man's
Guide to Albyn (with Lewis Grassic Gibbon) (1934); At the
Sign of the Thistle: A Collection of Essays (1934);
Charles Doughty and the Need for Heroic Poetry (1936);
Scottish Eccentrics (1936, 2nd edition 1972); Scotland and
the Question of a Popular Front Against Fascism and War
(1938); The Islands of Scotland (1939); Lucky Poet (1943,
2nd edition 1972); Cunninghame Graham (1952); The Politics
and Poetry of Hugh MacDiarmid (1952); Francis George Scott
(1955); Burns Today and Tomorrow (1959); David Hume (1962);
The Man of (almost) Independent Mind (1962); The Ugly
Birds Without Wings (1962); When the Rat-Race is Over
(1962); Sydney Goodsir Smith (1963); The Company I've Kept
(1966); Celtic Nationalism (other sections by Owen Dudley
Edwards, Gwynford Evans and Ioan Rhys) (1968); The Uncanny
Scot, ed. Kenneth Buthlay (1968); Selected Essays, ed.
Duncan Glen (1969); The MacDiarmids. A Conversation (with
Duncan Glen) (1970); A Political Speech (1972).
Edited: Northern Numbers (Three series 1920, 1921 and
1922); Robert Burns 1759-1796 (1926); Living Scottish Poets
(1931); The Golden Treasury of Scottish Poetry (1940);
William Soutar. Collected Poems (1948); Robert Burns. Poems
(1949); Selections from the Poems of William Dunbar (1952);
Selected Poems of William Dunbar (1955); Robert Burns.
Love Songs (1962); Henryson (1973). *Magazines edited:* The
Scottish Chapbook (1922-23); The Scottish Nation (1923);
The Northern Review (1924); The Voice of Scotland (1938-39,
1945-49, 1955-58).

CORRIE, Joe (1894-1968)
Poetry: Rebel Poems (1932); The Image o' God (1937);
Poems (1955). Also many plays.

KERR, Roderick Watson (1895-1960)
Poetry: Annus Mirabilis (1924); The Polite Educator (1925).

JEFFREY, William (1896-1946)
Poetry: Prometheus Returns (1921); The Wise Men Come to
Town (1923); The Nymph (1924); The Doom of Atlas (1926);
The Lamb of Lomond (1926); Mountain Songs (1928); The
Golden Stag (1932); Eagle of Coruisk (1933); Fantasia Written
in an Industrial Town (1933); Sea Glimmer (1947); Selected
Poems, ed. Alexander Scott (1951).

SOUTAR, William (1898-1943)
Poetry: Gleanings by an Undergraduate (1923); Conflict (1931);
Seeds in the Wind (1933, enlarged and revised 1943, and
illustrated edition 1948); The Solitary Way (1934); Brief
Words (1935); Poems in Scots (1935); A Handful of Earth
(1936); Riddles in Scots (1937); In the Time of Tyrants
(1939); But the Earth Abideth (1943); The Expectant Silence
(1944); Collected Poems, ed. Hugh MacDiarmid (1948); Poems
in Scots and English, ed. W.R. Aitken (1961). *Prose:* Diaries
of a Dying Man, ed. Alexander Scott (1954).

ORR, Christine (1899-1963)
Poetry: The Loud-Speaker (1928).

STUART, Alice V. (1899)
Poetry: The Far Calling (1944); The Dark Tarn (1953); The
Door Between (1963); The Unquiet Tide (1971). *Prose:* David
Gray. The Poet of the Luggie (1961). *Edited:* Voice and
Verse (with Charles Graves) (forthcoming 1974). *Magazine
edited:* The New Athenian Broadsheet (co-editor 1947-51).

THOMSON, David Cleghorn (1900-   )
Poetry: Far and Few (1923); Doges in the Ice-box (1928);
The Hidden Path: Poems 1922-1942 (1943); I Would be Acolyte
(1960). *Edited:* Scotland in Quest of her Youth (1932).
Magazine edited: Saltire Review (1960-1961).

MACLAREN, Hamish (1901-   )
Poetry: Sailor with Banjo (1929).

MACLEOD, Joseph ("Adam Drinan") (1903)
Poetry: The Ecliptic (1930); Foray of Centaurs (1931);
The Cove (1940); The Men of the Rocks (1942); The Ghosts
of the Strath (1943); Women of the Happy Island (1944);
The Passage of the Torch (1951); Script from Norway
(1953); An Old Olive Tree (1971). *Prose:* Beauty and the
Beast (1927); Why Not the Theatre? (1935); Overture to
Cambridge (1936); The New Soviet Theatre (1943); Actors
Cross the Volga (1946); A Job at the B.B.C. (1947); A
Soviet Theatre Sketch Book (1951); A Short History of
the British Theatre (1958); People of Florence (1968);
The Sisters d'Aranyi (1969). *Magazine edited:* The
Cherwell (1934).

MACKIE, A.D. (1904)
Poetry: Poems in Two Tongues (1928); Sing a Sang o'
Scotland (1944); A Call from Warsaw (1944); The Book of
MacNib (1957); Donald's Dive (1971); To Duncan Glen
(1971). *Prose:* Edinburgh (1951); Gentle Like a Dove
(1952); The Hearts (1959); Industrial History of
Edinburgh (1963); Scottish Pageantry (1967); The Scotch
Comedians (1973); The Scotch Whisky Drinker's
Companion (1973). *Newspapers and magazine edited:*
Edinburgh Evening Dispatch (1946-54); Lines Review
(nos. 16, 17, 1960-61); Edinburgh Weekly (1966).

MONTGOMERIE, William (1904)
Poetry: Via (1933); Squared Circle (1934). *Edited:*
Scottish Nursery Rhymes (with Norah Montgomerie) (1946);
New Judgments. Robert Burns (1947); Sandy Candy and
other Scottish Nursery Rhymes (with Norah Montgomerie)
(1948); The Well at the World's End: folk tales of
Scotland (with Norah Montgomerie) (1956); Hogarth Book
of Scottish Nursery Rhymes (with Norah Montgomerie)
(1964); A Book of Scottish Nursery Rhymes (with Norah
Montgomerie) (1965).

ANNAND, J.K. (1908)
Poetry: Sing it Aince for Pleisure (1965); Two Voices
(1968); Elegy on the Depairture o Mary Queen o Scots til
her Kinrick o Scotland (translated from the French of
Pierre de Ronsard) (1971); Twice for Joy (1973); Poems
and Translations (forthcoming). *Edited:* Early Lyrics by
Hugh MacDiarmid (1968). *Magazines edited:* The Broughton
Magazine (1925-26); The Rebel Student (1929); Lines
Review (nos. 14, 15, 1958-59); Lallans (1973-continuing).

BOLTON, Deric (1908)
Poetry: A View from Ben More (1972); Glasgow Central Station
(1972); The Wild Uncharted Country (1973).

BRUCE, George (1909)
Poetry: Sea Talk (1944); Selected Poems (1947); Landscapes
and Figures (1967); The Collected Poems of George Bruce (1970).
Prose: Scottish Sculpture (with T.S. Halliday) (1946); Neil
Miller Gunn (1971); A History of the Pitlochry Festival
Theatre (1972); City of Edinburgh (1973); Anne Redpath
(forthcoming 1974). *Edited:* The Exiled Heart by Maurice
Lindsay (1957); Scottish Poetry 1-6 (with Maurice Lindsay and
Edwin Morgan) (1966-1972); The Scottish Literary Revival. An
anthology of twentieth-century poetry (1968).

"GARIOCH, Robert" (Robert Garioch Sutherland) (1909)
Poetry: 17 Poems for 6d (with Sorley Maclean) (1940); Chuckies
on the Cairn (1949); The Masque of Edinburgh (1954); George
Buchanan's "Jephthah" and "The Baptist" (translated) (1959);
Selected Poems (1966); The Big Music (1971); Doktor Faust
in Rose Street (1973). *Prose:* Two Men and a Blanket (forth-
coming). *Edited:* New Scottish Poets (forthcoming).
Editorial Adviser Scottish International (1968-1974).

KINCAID, John (1909)
Poetry: Measures for Masses (1944); Time of Violence (1945);
Setterday Nicht Symphonie (1948); Foursom Reel (with George
Todd, F.J. Anderson and "Thurso Berwick", pseud. Robert Morris
Blythman) (1949); The Prince (1952).

MACCAIG, Norman (1910)
Poetry: Far Cry (1943); The Inward Eye (1946); Riding Lights
(1955); The Sinai Sort (1957); A Common Grace (1960); A Round
of Applause (1962); Measures (1965); Surroundings (1966);
Rings on a Tree (1968); A Man in my Position (1969); Selected
Poems (1971); The White Bird (1973); The World's Room (forthcoming 1974). Represented in The Penguin Modern Poets No.21
(1972). There is a MidNag Poster Poem (No.8) of MacCaig's
poem "Sunset Ploughing" with graphics by Enrico Equi. *Edited:*
Honour'd Shade (1959); Contemporary Scottish Verse 1959-1969
(with Alexander Scott) (1970).

MACLEAN, Sorley (Somhairle MacGhill Eathain) (1911)
Poetry: 17 Poems for 6d (with Robert Garioch) (1940);
Dàin do Eimhir (1943); Four Points of a Saltire (with
Stuart MacGregor, William Neill and George Campbell Hay)
(1970). Poems from Poems to Eimhir by Sorley Maclean
translated into English by Iain Crichton Smith (1971).

HENDRY, J.F. (1912)
Poetry: The Bombed Happiness (1942); The Orchestral
Mountain (1943). *Prose:* The Blackbird of Ospo. Stories
of Jugoslavia (1945); Fernie Brae: a Scottish Childhood
(1947); Verlon and the new image (1965). *Edited:*
Albannach. A little anthology of 1938 Scots poetry
(with C.J. Russell) (1938); The New Apocalypse (1939);
The White Horseman (with H. Treece) (1941); Scottish
Short Stories (with T. Hendry) (1943); The Crown and the
Sickle (with H. Treece) (1944); The Penguin Book of
Scottish Short Stories (1970).

TREMAYNE, Sydney (1912)
Poetry: For Whom there is no Spring (1946); Time and
the Wind (1948); The Hardest Freedom (1951); The Rock
and the Bird (1955); The Swans of Berwick (1962); The
Turning Sky (1969); Selected and New Poems (1973).
Magazine edited: Seven.

YOUNG, Douglas (1913-1973)
Poetry: Auntran Blads (1943); A Braird o' Thristles
(1947); Selected Poems (1950). *Plays:* The Puddocks
(translated) (1957); The Burdies (translated) (1959).
Prose: "Plastic Scots" and the Scottish Literary
Tradition (1947); The Use of Scots for Prose (1949);
Chasing an Ancient Greek (1950); Romanisation in
Scotland (1956); Edinburgh in the Age of Sir Walter Scott
(1965); St Andrews (1969); Scotland (1971). *Edited:*
Scottish Verse 1851-1951 (1952); Theognis (1961); Scots
Burds and Edinburgh Reviewers (1966).

GALLOWAY, Alexander (1914)
Poetry: War Poems in Scots (1942); The Lasting Vision
(1957).

SAUNDERS, R. Crombie (1914)
Poetry: XXI Poems (1955); The Year's Green Edge (1955).
Edited: Selected Poems of Hugh MacDiarmid (1944); A Guide
to the Fishing Inns of Scotland (1951). *Magazines and
newspaper edited:* Scottish Art and Letters (1944-48);
The Scottish Angler (1948-53); Scots Independent (1953-54).

TODD, Ruthven (1914)
Poetry: Ten Poems (1940); Until Now (1942); The Acreage of
the Heart (1944); The Planet in My Hand (1946); A Mantelpiece
of Shells (1954); Garland for the Winter Solstice (1961).
Prose: Over the Mountain (novel) (1939); The Lost Traveller
(1943); Tracks in the Snow (1946); William Blake, the artist
(1971). *Edited:* Christopher Smart. A Song to David (1947);
William Blake. Poems (1949).

FRASER, G.S. (1915)
Poetry: The Fatal Landscape (1941); Home Town Elegy (1944);
The Traveller Has Regrets (1948); Leaves Without a Tree
(1953); Conditions (1969). *Prose:* The Modern Writer and his
World (1953); W.B. Yeats (1954); Scotland (photographed by
Edwin Smith) (1955); Dylan Thomas (1957); Vision and Rhetoric
(1959); Ezra Pound (1960); Lawrence Durrell (1968); Metre,
Rhyme and Free Verse (1970); Lawrence Durrell (1970).
Edited: Springtime. An anthology (with I. Fletcher) (1953);
Poetry Now (1956); Robert Burns (1960); John Keats, Odes.
A Casebook (1971).

HAY, George Campbell (Deòrsa Caimbeul Hay) (1915)
Poetry: Fuaran Slèibh (1947); O Na Ceithir Àirdean (1952);
Wind on Loch Fyne (1948); Four Points of a Saltire (with
Stuart MacGregor, William Neill and Sorley Maclean (1970).

SMITH, Sydney Goodsir (1915)
Poetry: Skail Wind (1941); The Wanderer (1943); The Deevil's
Waltz (1946); Selected Poems (1947); Under the Eildon Tree
(1948); So Late into the Night (1952); Cokkils (1953);
Omens (1955); Orpheus and Eurydice (1955); Figs and Thistles
(1959); The Vision of the Prodigal Son (1960); Kynd Kittock's
Land (1965); Fifteen Poems and a Play (1969); Gowdspink in
Reekie (forthcoming 1974). *Verse Drama:* The Wallace (1960).
Prose: A Short Introduction to Scottish Literature (1951);

Carotid Cornucopius (1947, revised enlarged edition 1964).
Edited: Robert Fergusson 1750-1774 (1952); Gavin Douglas,
a selection from his poetry (1959); Hugh MacDiarmid: a
festschrift (with K.D. Duval) (1962); The Merry Muses of
Caledonia (with De Lancey Ferguson and James Barke) (1965);
A Choice of Burns's Poems and Songs (1966). *Magazine
edited:* Lines Review (Nos. 7-12, 1955-56).

LAW, T.S. (1916)
Poetry: Whit Tyme in the Day (1948). *Edited:* Homage to
John Maclean (with "Thurso Berwick", pseud. Robert Morris
Blythman) (1973).

DOW, Alexander (1917)
Poetry: The New Rigged Ship (1950); Twinty Canticles (1952).

GRAHAM, W.S. (1918)
Poetry: Cage Without Grievance (1942); The Seven Journeys
(1944); 2nd Poems (1945); The White Threshold (1949);
The Nightfishing (1955); Malcolm Mooney's Land (1970).
Represented in The Penguin Modern Poets No.17 (1970).

LINDSAY, Maurice (1918)
Poetry: The Advancing Day (1940); Perhaps To-morrow (1941);
Predicament (1942); No Crown for Laughter (1943); The
Enemies of Love (1946); Hurlygush (1948); At the Wood's
Edge (1950); Ode for St Andrews Night (1951); The Exiled
Heart(ed. George Bruce) (1957); Snow Warning (1962); One
Later Day (1964); This Business of Living (1968);
Comings and Goings (1971); Selected Poems 1942-1972 (1973).
Prose: A Pocket Guide to Scottish Culture (1947); The
Scottish Renaissance (1949); The Lowlands of Scotland:
Glasgow and the North (1953 and revised second edition
1973); Robert Burns (1954 and revised edition 1968); The
Lowlands of Scotland: Edinburgh and the South (1956);
Clyde Waters (1958); The Burns Encyclopedia (1959 and
enlarged and revised edition 1970); By Yon Bonnie Banks
(1961); The Discovery of Scotland (1964); The Eye is
Delighted: Some Romantic Travellers in Scotland (1971);
Portrait of Glasgow (1972). *Edited:* Sailing Tomorrow's
Seas (1944); Modern Scottish Poetry (1946 and revised
second edition 1966); No Scottish Twilight (with Fred
Urquhart) (1947); Selected Poems by Sir Alexander Gray

(1948); Selected Poems of Sir David Lyndsay of the Mount
(1948); Selected Poems of Marion Angus (with Helen B.
Cruickshank) (1950); John Davidson: a Selection of his Poems
(1961); Scottish Poetry 1-6 (with George Bruce and Edwin
Morgan) (1966-72); Scottish Poetry 7 (with Alexander Scott
and Roderick Watson) (forthcoming 1974); A Book of Scottish
Verse (re-edited 1967); Voices of our Kind (consultant
editor 1971); Scotland: An Anthology (forthcoming 1974).
Magazines edited: Poetry Scotland (1943-49); Scots Review
(with Alexander Scott) (1950-51).

"RITCHIE, Crae" (Rhoda Fraser) (1918-1970)
Poetry: Come in World (1963); Confrontation (1973).

SCOTT, Tom (1918)
Poetry: Seeven Poems o Maister Francis Villon (1953);
An Ode til New Jerusalem (1956); The Ship (1963); At the
Shrine o the Unkent Sodger (1968); Musins and Murgeonins
(forthcoming). *Prose:* Dunbar: A Critical Exposition of the
Poems (1966); Tales of King Robert the Bruce (1969); True
Thomas (1971). *Edited:* The Oxford Book of Scottish Verse
(with John MacQueen) (1966); Late Mediaeval Scots Poets
(1967); The Penguin Book of Scottish Verse (1970).
Magazine edited: Lines Review (No.13, 1957).

SENIOR, Charles (1918)
Poetry: Selected Poems (1966); Harbingers (1968).

"BERWICK, Thurso" (Robert Morris Blythman) (1919)
Poetry: Fowrsom Reel (with John Kincaid, George Todd and
F.J. Anderson) (1949). *Edited:* Sangs o' the Stane (1951);
Ding Dong Dollar (1961-63); Rebel Ceilidh Song-book '67
(1967); Homage to John Maclean (with T.S. Law) (1973).

HENDERSON, Hamish (1919)
Poetry: Ballads of World War II (1948); Elegies for the Dead
in Cyrenaica (1948).

MORGAN, Edwin (1920)
Poetry: The Vision of Cathkin Braes (1952); Beowulf
(translated) (1952); The Cape of Good Hope (1955); Poems
from Eugenio Montale (1959); Sovpoems (1961);
Starryveldt (1965); Scotch Mist (1965); Sealwear (1966);
Emergent Poems (1967); The Second Life (1968); Gnomes
(1968); Proverbfolder (1969); Twelve Songs (1970); The
Horseman's Word (1970); Selected Poems. Sándor Weöres
(translated) (Also prints Selected Poems. Ferenc
Juhasz, translated by David Wevill) (1970); The
Dolphin's Song (1971); Glasgow Sonnets (1972);
Instamatic Poems (1972); Wi the Haill Voice: 25 poems
by Vladimir Mayakovsky (translated) (1972); From
Glasgow to Saturn (1973); The Whittrick (1973).
Represented in The Penguin Modern Poets No.15 (1969).
Nuspeak 8 was given over to a group of visual poems by
Edwin Morgan (1973). *Prose:* Essays (forthcoming 1974).
Edited: Collins Albatross Book of Longer Poems (1963);
Scottish Poetry 1-6 (with George Bruce and Maurice
Lindsay); Poems by Alan Hayton, Stephen Mulrine, Colin
Kirkwood, Robert Tait (1967); Penguin New English
Dramatists 14 (1970). *Editorial Adviser* Scottish
International (1968-1974).

SCOTT, Alexander (1920)
Poetry: The Latest in Elegies (1949); Selected Poems
(1950); Mouth Music (1954); Cantrips (1968); Greek
Fire (1971); Double Agent (1972); Selected Poems
1943-1973 (forthcoming 1974). *Plays:* Prometheus 48
(1948); Untrue Thomas (1952); Shetland Yarn (1954);
Prose: Still Life: William Soutar 1898-1943 (1958);
The MacDiarmid Makars 1923-1972 (1972). *Edited:*
Selected Poems of William Jeffrey (1951); The Poems of
Alexander Scott c.1530-c.1584 (1952); Diaries of a
Dying Man by William Soutar (1954); Contemporary
Scottish Verse 1959-1969 (with Norman MacCaig) (1970);
The Hugh MacDiarmid Anthology (with Michael Grieve)
(1972); Neil M. Gunn: The Man and the Writer (with
Douglas Gifford) (1973); Scottish Poetry 7 (with Maurice
Lindsay and Roderick Watson) (forthcoming 1974).
Magazines edited: North-East Review (1945-46); Scots
Review (with Maurice Lindsay) (1950-51); Saltire Review
(1954-57, jointly in 1956-57).

BROWN, George Mackay (1921)
Poetry: The Storm (1954); Loaves and Fishes (1959); The Year
of the Whale (1965); The Five Voyages of Arnor (1966); Twelve
Poems (1968); Fisherman with Ploughs (1971); Poems New and
Selected (1971). Represented in The Penguin Modern Poets No.21
(1972). *Prose:* A Calendar of Love (stories) (1967); A Time
to Keep (stories) (1969); An Orkney Tapestry (essays, etc)
(1969); Greenvoe (novel) (1972); Magnus (novel) (1973);
Hawkfall (stories) (forthcoming 1974); The Two Fiddlers
(stories for children) (forthcoming 1974). *Play:* A Spell for
Green Corn (1970).

COOK. R.L. (1921)
Poetry: Hebrides Overture (1948); Within the Tavern Caught
(1952); Sometimes a Word (1963). *Magazines edited:* Fleet
Poetry Broadsheet (1944-46); The New Athenian Broadsheet
(co-editor 1947-48); Windfall (co-editor 1955).

THOMSON, Derick (Ruaraidh MacThómais) (1921)
Poetry: An Dealbh Briste (1951); Eadar Samhradh Is Foghar
(1967); An Rathad Cian (1970). Lines Review No.39 was
devoted to "The Far Road and other poems" by Derick Thomson
(December 1971). *Prose:* The Gaelic Sources of Macpherson's
"Ossian" (1952); An Introduction to Gaelic Poetry (1974).
Edited: Branwen Uerch Lyr (1961); Edward Lhwyd in the Scottish
Highlands 1699-1700 (with J.L. Campbell) (1963); The Future
of the Highlands (with Ian Grimble) (1968). *Magazines
edited:* Gairm (1951-continuing); Scottish Gaelic Studies
(1961-74).

NEILL, William (1922)
Poetry: Scotland's Castle (1969); Poems (1970); Four Points
of a Saltire (with Stuart MacGregor, George Campbell Hay and
Sorley Maclean) (1970); Despatches Home (1972); Buile Shuibhne
(translated) (forthcoming 1974). *Magazine edited:* Catalyst
(1968-70).

WOOD, Kenneth (1923)
Poetry: Poems (1970).

MORRICE, Ken (1924)
Poetry: Prototype (1965)

FINLAY, Ian Hamilton (1925)
Books and Booklets: The Sea-Bed and Other Stories, Alna
Press (1958); The Dancers Inherit The Party, Migrant
Press (1960; 2nd edition Migrant Press 1962); Glasgow
Beasts, An a Burd, Wild Hawthorn Press (1961; 2nd edition
February 1962; 3rd edition June 1962; 4th edition
December 1962; 5th edition Fulcrum Press 1965);
Concertina, Wild Hawthorn Press (1962); Rapel, Wild
Hawthorn Press (1963); Canal Stripe Series 3, Wild Hawthorn
Press (1964); Canal Stripe Series 4, Wild Hawthorn Press
(1964); Telegrams from My Windmill, Wild Hawthorn Press
(1964); Ocean Stripe Series 2, Wild Hawthorn Press (1965);
Ocean Stripe Series 3, Wild Hawthorn Press (1965); Cythera,
Wild Hawthorn Press (1965); Und Alles Blieb Wie Es
War ... (one-act plays, translated into German), Universal
Editions (1965); Autumn Poem, Wild Hawthorn Press (1966);
6 Small Pears for Eugen Gomringer, Wild Hawthorn Press
(1966); 6 Small Songs in 3's, Wild Hawthorn Press (1966);
Tea-leaves and Fishes, Wild Hawthorn Press (1966); 4 Sails,
Wild Hawthorn Press (1966); Headlines Eaveslines, Openings
Press (1967); Stonechats, Wild Hawthorn Press (1967);
Ocean Stripe Series 5, Tarasque Press (1967); Canal Game,
Fulcrum Press (1967); The Collected Coaltown of Callange
Tri-kai, Screwpacket Press (1968); Air Letters, Tarasque
Press (1968); The Blue and The Brown Poems, Jargon Press,
with Atlantic Richfield (1968); The Dancers Inherit The
Party, Fulcrum Press (1969: 3rd edition wrongly described
as 'First'); 3/3's, Wild Hawthorn Press (1969); A Boatyard,
Wild Hawthorn Press (1969); Lanes, Wild Hawthorn Press
(1969); Wave, Wild Hawthorn Press (1969); Rhymes For
Lemons, Wild Hawthorn Press (1970); 'Fishing News' News,
Wild Hawthorn Press (1970); Ceolfrith 5, Ceolfrith Press
(1970); 30 Signatures to Silver Catches, Tarasque Press
(1971); Poems to Hear and See, The Macmillan Company, New
York (1971); A Sailor's Calendar, Something Else Press,
U.S.A. (1971); The Olsen Excerpts, Verlag Udo Breger (1971);
A Memory of Summer, Wild Hawthorn Press (1971); From 'An
Inland Garden', Wild Hawthorn Press (1971); Evening/Sail 2,
Wild Hawthorn Press (1971); The Weed Boat Masters Ticket,
Preliminary Test (Part Two), Wild Hawthorn Press (1971);
Sail/Sundial, Wild Hawthorn Press (1972); Jibs, Wild
Hawthorn Press (1972); Butterflies, Wild Hawthorn Press
(1973); A Family, Wild Hawthorn Press (1973); Straiks (with

Simon Cutts and Sydney McK. Glen), Wild Hawthorn Press (1973);
Exercise X (with George L. Thomson), Wild Hawthorn Press
(1973); Honey By The Water, Black Sparrow Press (1973).
Cards and Folding Cards: Star/Steer, Brighton Festival
publication (1967); 3 Blue Lemons, Wild Hawthorn Press (1967);
2 From the Yard of ..., Wild Hawthorn Press (1967); Sea-
poppy 1, Wild Hawthorn Press (1968); Sea-poppy 2, Wild
Hawthorn Press (1968); The Land's Shadows, Wild Hawthorn Press
(1968); From 'The Analects of Fishing News', Wild Hawthorn
Press (1968); From 'The Illuminations of Fishing News', Wild
Hawthorn Press (1969); From 'TA MYOIKA of Fishing News',
Wild Hawthorn Press (1969); Net/Planet, Wild Hawthorn Press
(1969); Barges (with Margot Sandeman), Wild Hawthorn Press
(1969); Point-to-Point (with Jim Nicholson), Wild Hawthorn
Press (1969); 4 Sails (photograph by J.W. Lucas), Wild
Hawthorn Press (1969); Xmas Star (Christmas Card, with John
Furnival), Wild Hawthorn Press (1969); Skylarks, Wild Hawthorn
Press (1970); Valses Pour Piano, Wild Hawthorn Press (1970);
Arcadian Sundials (with Margot Sandeman), Wild Hawthorn Press
(1970); From 'The Metamorphoses of Fishing News', Wild Haw-
thorn Press (1970); A Waterlily Pool (with Ian Gardner), Wild
Hawthorn Press (1970); Still Life With Lemon, Wild Hawthorn
Press (1970); Les Hirondelles (with Ron Costley), Wild Haw-
thorn Press (1970); A Patch ..., Wild Hawthorn Press (1970);
Sheaves, Wild Hawthorn Press (1970); A Use for Old Beehives
(with Richard Demarco), Wild Hawthorn Press (1970); Xmas Rose
(Christmas Card, with John Furnival), Wild Hawthorn Press
(1970); Zulu 'Chieftain' (with A Doyle Moore), Wild Hawthorn
Press (1971); A Sea Street Anthology (photograph by Gloria
Wilson), Wild Hawthorn Press (1971); Homage to Donald McGill,
Wild Hawthorn Press (1971); Flags, Wild Hawthorn Press (1971);
The Sign of The Nudge, Wild Hawthorn Press (1971); The Harbour
(photograph by Diane Tammes), Wild Hawthorn Press (1971);
The Old Nobby (photograph by Diane Tammes), Wild Hawthorn
Press (1971); Sails/Waves 1 (with Ron Costley), Wild Hawthorn
Press (1971); Sails/Waves 2 (with Ron Costley), Wild Hawthorn
Press (1971); I Saw Three Ships (with Ron Costley), Wild
Hawthorn Press (1971); Is There a Ship ..., Wild Hawthorn
Press (1971); A Heart-Shape (with Ron Costley), Wild Hawthorn
Press (1971); Birch-Bark (photograph by Diane Tammes), Wild
Hawthorn Press (1971); Daisies (with Ian Gardner), Wild Haw-
thorn Press (1971); Book-Flag (with Ron Costley), Wild Haw-
thorn Press (1971); The Land's Shadows (with Michael Harvey,
as a Christmas Card for Daedalus Press)(1971); Kite (New Year
Card), Wild Hawthorn Press (1971); Tree-Shells (with Ian
Gardner), Wild Hawthorn Press (1971); Catches (with Margot
Sandeman), Wild Hawthorn Press (1971); Unicorn (photograph by

Diane Tammes), Wild Hawthorn Press (1971); Elegy for
Whimbrel and Petrel (with Ian Gardner), Sepia Press (1971);
Xmas Morn (Christmas Card, with Michael Harvey), Wild
Hawthorn Press (1971); Homage to E.A. Hornel, Wild Hawthorn
Press (1972); Fl (photograph by John Roberts), Wild
Hawthorn Press (1972); The End ... (with Ian Gardner), Wild
Hawthorn Press (1972); Homage to Seurat (with Ron Costley),
Wild Hawthorn Press (1972); Homage to Walter Reekie's Ring
Netters (with Ron Costley), Wild Hawthorn Press (1972);
Kite-Estuary Model (with Ian Gardner), Wild Hawthorn Press
(1972); Iron Ship (with Ian Gardner), Wild Hawthorn Press
(1972); Homage to Jonathan Williams (with Michael Harvey),
Wild Hawthorn Press (1972); Blue/Water's/Bark, Wild Haw-
thorn Press (1972); Homage to Kandinsky (with Ron Costley),
Wild Hawthorn Press (1972); Homage to Kahnweiler (with
Stuart Barrie), Wild Hawthorn Press (1972); Tye/Cringle
Christmas Card for 1972, Wild Hawthorn Press; Der Tag (with
Ron Costley), Wild Hawthorn Press (1972); Estuary Cupboards
(with Michael Harvey), Wild Hawthorn Press (1972); The
Sea's Waves (with Stuart Barrie), Wild Hawthorn Press (1972);
Trim Here (with Michael Harvey), Wild Hawthorn Press (1973);
Mid-Pacific Elements, Wild Hawthorn Press (1973); Tea-Cards,
Set of 3 (with Simon Cutts), Wild Hawthorn Press (1973);
Bath Roundels (with George Oliver), Wild Hawthorn Press
(1973); Homage to Pop Art (with Sydney McK. Glen), Wild
Hawthorn Press (1973); Mower is Less, Wild Hawthorn Press
(1973); Homage to Victor Silvester (with Michael Harvey),
Wild Hawthorn Press (1973); Wild Hawthorn Weapons Series
No.1 (with Susan Goodricke), Wild Hawthorn Press (1973);
Harlequin (Detail) (with Karl Torok), Wild Hawthorn Press
(1973); Schiff (with Ron Costley), Wild Hawthorn Press
(1973); Landscape/Interior (with Karl Torok), Wild Hawthorn
Press (1973); 'A Calm in a Tea-Cup' (with Richard Demarco),
Wild Hawthorn Press (1973). *Poem/Prints:* Poster Poem (Le
Circus), Wild Hawthorn Press (1964); Summer Poem (with Jim
Nicholson), Wild Hawthorn Press (1966); Acrobats, Tarasque
Press (1966); Star/Steer, Tarasque Press (1966); Sea-poppy 1
(with Alistair Cant), Tarasque Press (1966); Ajar, Wild
Hawthorn Press (1967); La Belle Hollandaise (with Herbert
Rosenthal), Wild Hawthorn Press (1967); Land/Sea (with
Herbert Rosenthal), Wild Hawthorn Press (1967); Marine (with
Patrick Caulfield), Wild Hawthorn Press (1968); Sea-poppy 2,
Wild Hawthorn Press (1968); Poem/print No.11 (with John
Furnival), Wild Hawthorn Press (1969); Seams, Wild Hawthorn
Press (1969); Evening/Sail, Wild Hawthorn Press (1970);
Catameringue (with Peter Grant), Wild Hawthorn Press (1970);
Poem/print No.14 (with John Furnival), Wild Hawthorn Press

(1970); The Little Seamstress (with Richard Demarco), Wild
Hawthorn Press (1970); Homage to Mozart (with Ron Costley),
Wild Hawthorn Press (1970); Scottish Zulu (with David Button),
Wild Hawthorn Press (1970); Shenval Christmas Poem/print
(1971); Sailing Barge Redwing (with Ian Gardner), Wild
Hawthorn Press (1971); A Rock Rose (with Richard Demarco),
Wild Hawthorn Press (1971); Archangel (with Sydney Glen),
Wild Hawthorn Press (1971); Seashells (with Ian Proctor),
Wild Hawthorn Press (1971); The Little Drummer Boy (with Ron
Costley), Wild Hawthorn Press (1971); Homage to Vuillard
(with Michael Harvey), Wild Hawthorn Press (1971); Prinz
Eugen (with Ron Costley), Wild Hawthorn Press (1972); Sail
Wholemeal (with Jim Nicholson), Wild Hawthorn Press (1972);
Homage to Modern Art (with Jim Nicholson), Wild Hawthorn
Press (1972); Illustrious (Aircraft Carrier sculpture/project,
with Richard England), Wild Hawthorn Press (1972); The
Washington Fountain (with Karl Torok), Wild Hawthorn Press
(1972); Topiary Aircraft Carrier (with Ian Gardner), Wild
Hawthorn Press (1972); Necktank (with Michael Harvey), Wild
Hawthorn Press (1973); Arcadia (with George Oliver), Wild
Hawthorn Press (1973); Gourd (with Ron Costley), Wild Hawthorn
Press (1973); *Other Publications:* Standing Poem 1, Wild
Hawthorn Press (1963); Standing Poem 2, Wild Hawthorn Press
(1965); Standing Poem 3, Wild Hawthorn Press (1965); First
Suprematist Standing Poem, Wild Hawthorn Press (1965);
Earthship, Wild Hawthorn Press (1965); Futura 7, Editions
Hansjorg Mayer (1965); Arcady, Tarasque Press (1968); After
the Russian, Openings Press (1969); Errata (with David Button),
Wild Hawthorn Press (1970); The Weed Boat Masters Ticket
Preliminary Test (Part One), Tarasque Press (1970); Boats of
Letters, Tarasque Press (1970); Glossary (with Richard
Demarco), Wild Hawthorn Press (1971); Street Handout, Ceolfrith
Press (1971); Spiral Binding (with Ron Costley), Wild Hawthorn
Press (1972); D1 (with Michael Harvey), Wild Hawthorn Press
(1972); Copyright (with Ron Costley), Wild Hawthorn Press
(1973); Stationery (with David Button), Wild Hawthorn Press
(1973); Family Group--Levens Hall Topiary (with Karl Torok),
Wild Hawthorn Press (1973). *Works in public places:* Sundials:
Biggar, Kelso, University of Kent, Canterbury; Neon mural
poem: State Museum, Lodz, Poland. *Works in process of being
built:* Cythera (extended poem in ceramic and concrete), Royal
Botanic Gardens, Edinburgh; Land's Shadows, sundial, Aberdeen
Parks; Max Planck Institute (and surrounding gardens) project,
Stuttgart, Germany. *Edited:* Poor. Old. Tired. Horse. Poetry-
sheet (Issues 1-25).

MACKIE, Alastair (1925)
Poetry: Soundings (1966); Clytach (1972); At the Heich
Kirk-yaird (forthcoming 1974).

GOLD, Eric (1927)
Poetry: Poems (1969).

RIDDELL, Alan (1927)
Poetry: Beneath the Summer (1952); Majorcan Interlude
(1960); The Stopped Landscape (1968); Eclipse (1972).
Edited: Typewriter Art (forthcoming 1974). *Magazine
edited:* Lines Review (1952-55 and 1962-67).

SINGER, James Burns (1928-1964)
Poetry: The Gentle Engineer (1952); Still and All (1957);
The Collected Poems, ed. W.A.S. Keir (1970). *Prose:*
Living Silver (1957). *Edited:* Five Centuries of Polish
Poetry 1450-1950 (with Jerzy M. Peterkiewicz) (1960).

SMITH, Iain Crichton (Iain Mac A' Ghobhainn) (1928)
Poetry: The Long River (1955); "White Noon" in New Poets
1959 (with Karen Gershon and Christopher Levenson) ed.
Edwin Muir (1959); Thistles and Roses (1961); Deer on the
High Hills (1962); The Law and the Grace (1965); Biobuill
is Sanasan-reice (1965); At Helensburgh (1968); Three
Regional Voices (with Michael Longley and Barry Tebb)
ed. Alan Tarling (1968); From Bourgeois Land (1969); Ben
Dorain by Duncan Ban Macintyre (translated) (1969);
Selected Poems (1970); Poems to Eimhir by Sorley Maclean
(translated) (1971); Love Poems and Elegies (1972); Hamlet
in Autumn (1972); Rabhdan is Rudan (1973); Orpheus (forth-
coming 1974). Lines Review No.29 is devoted to poetry by
Iain Crichton Smith (1969). Represented in The Penguin
Modern Poets No.21 (1972). *Prose:* Burn is Aran (short
stories) (1960); An Dubh is an Gorm (short stories) (1963);
Modern Gaelic Verse (1966); The Golden Lyric. An Essay
on the Poetry of Hugh MacDiarmid (1967); Consider the
Lilies (novel) (1968); The Last Summer (novel) (1969);
Survival Without Error (short stories) (1970); Iain Am
Measg Nan Reultan (children's book) (1970); Maighstirean
is Ministearan (short stories) (1970); My Last Duchess
(novel) (1971); The Black and the Red (short stories)
(1973); An t-Adhar Ameireaganach (short stories) (1973).

MCKILLOP, Menzies (1929)
Poetry: Poems (1969).

MACAULEY, Donald (Dòmhnall MacAmhlaigh)
Poetry: Seòbhrach Às A' Chlaich (1967).

BUCHAN, Tom (1931)
Poetry: Ikons (1957); Dolphins at Cochin (1969); Exorcism
(1972); Poems 1969-1972 (1972). *Magazines edited:* Scottish
International (July 1973-74); Aquarius (September 1973).

MACBETH, George (1932)
Poetry: A Form of Words (1954); Lecture to the Trainees
(1962); The Broken Places (1963); A Doomsday Book (1965);
The Twelve Hotels (1965); Missile Commander (1965); The
Calf (1965); The Humming-Birds (1965); The Colour of Blood
(1967); The Screens (1967); The Night of Stones (1968);
A War Quartet (1969); The Bamboo Nightingale (1970); The
Burning Cone (1970); Poems (1970); Two Poems (1970); The
Orlando Poems (1971); Collected Poems 1958-1970 (1971);
A Farewell (1972); Lusus (1972); Shrapnel (1973); Prayers
(1973); A Poet's Year (1973). Represented in The Penguin
Modern Poets No.6 (1964). *Prose:* My Scotland (1973); The
Transformation (1974). *Edited:* The Penguin Book of Sick
Verse (1963); The Penguin Book of Animal Verse (1965);
Poetry 1900 to 1965 (1967); The Penguin Book of Victorian
Verse (1969); Alfred Tennyson. The Falling Splendour. Poems
(1970).

MITCHELL, David (1932)
Poetry: Luvesangs and ithers (1956).

HARDIE, George (1933)
Poetry: Voice of the Curlew (1966); Poems (1969).
Magazine edited: The Chapman (with Walter Perrie) (1970-71).

GLEN, Duncan ("Ronald Eadie Munro") (1933)
Poetry: Stanes (1966); Idols: When Alexander our King
was dead (1967); Kythings (1969); Sunny Summer Sunday
Afternoon in the Park? (1969); Unnerneath the Bed (1970);
In Appearances (1971); Clydesdale (1971); Feres (1971);
A Journey Past (1972); A Cled Score (1974). *Prose:*
Hugh MacDiarmid: Rebel Poet and Prophet (1962); Hugh
MacDiarmid and the Scottish Renaissance (1964); The
Literary Masks of Hugh MacDiarmid (1964); Scottish Poetry
Now (1966); A Small Press and Hugh MacDiarmid (1970);
The MacDiarmids. A Conversation (with Hugh MacDiarmid)
(1970); The Individual and the Twentieth-Century Scottish
Literary Tradition (1971). *Edited:* Poems Addressed to
Hugh MacDiarmid (1967); Selected Essays of Hugh Mac-
Diarmid (1969); The Akros Anthology of Scottish Poetry
1965-70 (1970); Whither Scotland? (1971); Hugh MacDiarmid.
A Critical Survey (1972); A Bibliography of Scottish
Poets from Stevenson to 1974 (1974). *Magazines edited:*
Akros (1965-continuing); Knowe (1971).

CONN, Stewart (1936)
Poetry: Thunder in the Air (1967); The Chinese Tower
(1967); Stoats in the Sunlight (1968); An Ear to the
Ground (1972). *Plays:* The Burning (1973); In Transit
(1973); The Aquarium and other plays (forthcoming 1974).
Represented in Penguin New English Dramatists 14 (1970).
Edited: New Poems 1973-1974 (forthcoming 1974).

WHITE, Kenneth (1936)
Poetry: Wild Coal (1963); En Toute Candeur (1964); The
Cold Wind of Dawn (1966); The Most Difficult Area (1968);
André Breton. Selected Poems (translated) (1969); André
Breton. Ode to Charles Fourier (translated) (1969); Terre
de Diamant (forthcoming 1974). *Prose:* Letters from
Gourgonnel (1966); Cosmos (1970); Travels in the Drifting
Dawn (1972).

FULTON, Robin (1937)
Poetry: A Manner of Definition (1963); An Italian Quartet
(translated) (1966); Instances (1967); Blok's "Twelve"
(translated) (1968); Inventories (1969); Quarters (1970);
The Spaces Between the Stones (1971); The Man with the
Surbahar (1971); Selected Poems. Lars Gustafsson (translated) (1972); Gunnar Harding. They Killed Sitting Bull

(translated) (1973); Tree-Lines (forthcoming 1974); Tomas
Tranströmer (translated) (forthcoming 1974); Östen Sjöstrand
(translated) (forthcoming 1974). *Prose:* Contemporary Scottish
Poetry, Individuals and Contexts (forthcoming 1974).
Magazine edited: Lines Review (since No.24, Summer 1967-
continuing).

AITCHISON, James (1938)
Poetry: Sounds Before Sleep (1971).

JACKSON, Alan (1938)
Poetry: Underwater Wedding (1961); Sixpenny Poems (1962);
Well Ye Ken Noo (1963); All Fall Down (1965); The Worstest
Beast (1967); The Grim Wayfarer (1969); Idiots are Freelance
(1973). Represented in The Penguin Modern Poets No.12 (1968).
Prose: Lines Review No.37 (June 1971) was given over to
"The Knitted Claymore. An Essay on Culture and Nationalism"
by Alan Jackson.

MULRINE, Stephen (1938)
Poetry: Poems by Alan Hayton, Stephen Mulrine, Colin Kirkwood,
Robert Tait, ed. Edwin Morgan (with others as in title)
(1967); Poems (1971).

RANKIN, James (1939)
Poetry: 28 Poems (with Roderick Watson) (1964); Poems (1969).
Edited: The Ring of Words (with Alan MacGillivray) (1970).

CAMPBELL, Donald (1940)
Poetry: Poems (1971); Rhymes 'n Reasons (1972).

GORDON, Giles (1940)
Poetry: Landscape any Date (1963); Two and Two Make One (1966);
Two Elegies (1968); Eight Poems for Gareth (1970); Twelve
Poems for Callum (1972). *Prose:* Pictures from an Exhibition
(1970); The Umbrella Man (1971); About a Marriage (1972);
Girl with Red Hair (1974). *Edited:* Factions (with Alex.
Hamilton) (1974); New English Fiction (forthcoming 1974).
Magazine edited: New Saltire (with Michael Scott-Moncrieff)
(1961-62).

JOHNSTON, J. Laughton (1940)
Poetry: Meetings (1968).

MCGRATH, Tom (1940)
Poetry: The Buddha Poems (1973). *Magazines edited:*
International Times (1967-68); Glasgow University Magazine
(1971-72).

BLACK. David M. (1941)
Poetry: Rocklestrakes (1960); From the Mountain (1963);
Theory of Diet (1966); With Decorum (1967); A Dozen Short
Poems (1968); The Educators (1969); The Old Hag (1972);
The Happy Crow (forthcoming 1974). Represented in The
Penguin Modern Poets No.11 (1968). *Magazine edited:* Extra
Verse (1964-66).

MORRISON, David (1941)
Poetry: The Saxon Toon (1966); The White Hind (1968);
The Clay Yerd (1970); The Winter Aisling (1971); White
Witch, White Woman (1972); Paddy's Mairket (1973).
Prose: The Thorn that Cuts (1971); The Idealist and other
stories (1973); Hammer and Thistle (with Alan Bold)
(forthcoming 1974). *Edited:* Essays on Neil M. Gunn (1971);
Essays on Fionn MacColla (1973). *Magazine edited:* Scotia
(1970-72); Scotia Review (1972-continuing).

DUNN, Douglas (1942)
Poetry: Terry Street (1969); Backwaters (1971); The
Happier Life (1972); Love or Nothing (forthcoming 1974).
Edited: New Poems 1973 (1973); A Choice of Lord Byron's
Verse (forthcoming 1974); Contemporary Irish Writing
(with Michael Schmidt) (forthcoming 1974). *Magazine
edited:* Antaeus (No.12, 1973).

MACINTYRE, Lorn M. (1942)
Poetry: I Wait (1964). *Prose:* Blood and the Moon (novel)
(forthcoming 1974).

BOLD, Alan (1943)
Poetry: Society Inebrious (1965); The Voyage (1966); To Find
the New (1967); A Perpetual Motion Machine (1969); The State
of the Nation (1969); He will be greatly missed (1971); The
Auld Symie (1971); A Century of People (1971); A Pint of
Bitter (1971); A Lunar Event (1973). Represented in The
Penguin Modern Poets No.15 (1969). *Prose:* Hammer and Thistle
(with David Morrison) (forthcoming 1974). *Edited:* The Penguin
Book of Socialist Verse (1970); Landings (forthcoming 1974);
The Cambridge Book of English Verse 1939-74 (forthcoming 1974).
Magazines edited: Gambit (1963 and 1965); Rocket (1964-65).

TAIT, Robert (1943)
Poetry: Poems by Alan Hayton, Stephen Mulrine, Colin Kirkwood,
Robert Tait, ed. Edwin Morgan (with others as in title)
(1967). *Magazine edited:* Scottish International (1968-
August 1973).

WATSON, Roderick (1943)
Poetry: 28 Poems (with James Rankin) (1964); Poems (1970);
Trio: New Poets from Edinburgh (with Valerie Simmons and Paul
Mills) (1971). *Edited:* Scottish Poetry 7 (with Maurice
Lindsay and Alexander Scott) (forthcoming 1974).

CLARK, Thomas A. (1944)
Poetry: Down and Out in Tighnabruaich (1970); Some Particulars
(1971); Pointing Still (1974); The Garden (1974); Four Flowers
(1974). *Magazine edited:* Bo heem e um (1966-68).

LEONARD, Tom (1944)
Poetry: Six Glasgow Poems (1969); A Priest Came on at Merkland
Street (1970); Poems (1973). *Magazine edited:* Glasgow
University Magazine (1968-69).

MUNRO, Robin (1946)
Poetry: Shetland, Like the World (1973). *Magazine edited:*
New North (1967-68).

LOCHHEAD, Liz (1947)
Poetry: Memo for Spring (1972).

PERRIE, Walter (1949)
Poetry: Deidre (1971); Ulysses (1971). *Magazine edited:*
The Chapman (1970-71 with George Hardie) (1972-continuing).

GREIG, Andrew (1951)
Poetry: White Boats (with Catherine Lucy Czerkawska)
(1973)

SCOTTISH ANTHOLOGIES WITH TWENTIETH CENTURY
SCOTTISH POETRY

Northern Numbers, ed. C.M. Grieve (1920, second series
1921, third series 1922).

The Northern Muse, ed. John Buchan (1924).

Holyrood: A Garland of Modern Scots Poems, ed. W.H.
Hamilton (1929).

A Scots Garland: An Anthology of Scottish Vernacular
Verse, ed. Thomas Henderson (1931).

Living Scottish Poets, ed. C.M. Grieve (1931).

Oor Mither Tongue, ed. Ninian MacWhannell (1937).

Albannach: A Little Anthology of 1938 Scots Poetry,
ed. C.J. Russell and J.F. Hendry (1938).

The Golden Treasury of Scottish Poetry, ed. Hugh
MacDiarmid (1940).

Modern Scottish Poetry. An Anthology of the Scottish
Renaissance 1920-1945, ed. Maurice Lindsay (1946,
revised and extended second edition to the mid-sixties
1966).

A Scots Anthology, ed. John W. Oliver and J.C. Smith (1949).

Poets' Quair, ed. David Rintoul and J.B. Skinner (1950).

New Scots Poetry. A selection of short poems from the Festival of Britain Scots Poetry Competition (1952).

Scottish Verse 1851-1951, ed. Douglas Young (1952).

Honour'd Shade. An Anthology of New Scottish Poetry, ed. Norman MacCaig (1959).

Scottish Poetry Nos. 1-6, ed. George Bruce, Maurice Lindsay and Edwin Morgan (1966-72); No.7, ed. Maurice Lindsay, Alexander Scott and Roderick Watson (forthcoming 1974).

The Oxford Book of Scottish Verse, ed. John MacQueen and Tom Scott (1966).

A Book of Scottish Verse, new revised edition, ed. Maurice Lindsay (1967).

The Scottish Literary Revival: An anthology of twentieth-century poetry, ed. George Bruce (1968).

The Akros Anthology of Scottish Poetry 1965-70, ed. Duncan Glen (1970).

Contemporary Scottish Verse 1959-1969, ed. Norman MacCaig and Alexander Scott (1970).

The Penguin Book of Scottish Verse, ed. Tom Scott (1970).

The Ring of Words: An anthology of Scottish poetry for secondary schools, ed. Alan MacGillivray and James Rankin (1970).

Twelve Modern Scottish Poets, ed. Charles King (1971).

Voices of Our Kind, consultant ed. Maurice Lindsay (1971).

Seven New Voices. Poems by Derek Bowman, Catherine Lucy Czerkawska, Andrew Greig, Liz Lochhead, Brian McCabe, Mario Relich, David Walls, ed. John Schofield (1972).

New Scottish Poets, ed. Robert Garioch (forthcoming 1974).

SCOTTISH LITERARY MAGAZINES: A SELECT LIST

The Scottish Chapbook, ed. C.M. Grieve (1922-23).

The Modern Scot, ed. J.H. Whyte (1930-36)

The Voice of Scotland, ed. Hugh MacDiarmid (1938-39,
1945-49, 1955-58).

Poetry Scotland, ed. Maurice Lindsay (1943-49).

Gairm, ed. Derick Thomson and Finlay McDonald
and continuing Derick Thomson alone (1951-continuing).

Lines (Lines Review from No.4), various editors
(Alan Riddell; Sydney Goodsir Smith; Tom Scott;
J.K. Annand; Albert Mackie; Alan Riddell; and the
current editor Robin Fulton) (1952-continuing).

Saltire Review, various editors (Alexander Scott;
Alexander Scott and J.M. Reid; Alexander Reid; David
Cleghorn Thomson) (1954-61).

New Saltire, various editors (Giles Gordon and
Michael Scott-Moncrieff; Giles Gordon; Magnus Magnusson)
(1961-64).

The Glasgow Review, ed. Joseph Mulholland (1964-5 and
1972-continuing).

Akros, ed. Duncan Glen (1965-continuing).

Scottish International, ed. Robert Tait; and succeeded
by Tom Buchan (with Robert Garioch and Edwin Morgan
as Editorial Advisers throughout) (1968-74).

Scotia (Scotia Review from August 1972), ed. David
Morrison (1970-continuing).

Chapman, ed. George Hardie and Walter Perrie, then
Walter Perrie alone, and continuing Walter Perrie and
Joy Perrie (1970-continuing).

IN APPEARANCES. A SEQUENCE OF POEMS   Cloth / £1.15
". . . is already, in his late thirties, a very considerable poet. *In Appearances* is an eighty-page work
made up of connected and developing poem-clusters and
concluded by a ten-page imaginary autobiography. The
whole defines a highly articulated life-view . . . "
--Anne Cluysenaar, *Stand*.

CLYDESDALE. A SEQUENCE OF POEMS   Wrappers / £0.30
"A fine, sturdy, colloquial sequence about the history
and even pre-history of his home area in the context of
the building of a New Town."--Adrian Henri, *The Guardian*.

FERES. POEMS   Wrappers / Limited signed edition £1.25
"As a rule, Glen's colloquial Scots is highly success-
ful. He is to be congratulated for giving us some of
the best poems in Scots of the past twenty years."
--Thomas Crawford, *Lines Review*.

A CLED SCORE. POEMS   Cloth / £1.15
"He writes in an easy lallans style presenting ideas
that often challenge our complacency, but are seldom
obscure in the offputting way of the pedant. A large-
spirited lyricism is what we find in his reflective
autobiographical pieces like the final poem 'A Journey
Past' in which he considers the industrial legacy of
the Scottish central belt, but still feels optimism."
--Cuthbert Graham, *Aberdeen Press and Journal*.

Available, post paid in U.K. from
Akros Publications
14 Parklands Avenue, Penwortham, Preston
Lancashire, PR1 0QL

Akros, edited by Duncan Glen, has been appearing since the summer of 1965 and has established itself as a magazine firmly committed to a distinctive Scottish literature, but it has been an anti-parochial commitment which looks outwards as well as around Scotland. As early as no.5 *The Scotsman* wrote: "The handsomely produced July issue reads like a who's who in Scottish poetry today" and inevitably, with the support of so many established Scottish poets, the standard has been high. As Alexander Scott said on the publication of no.9, a special translation issue, "It is many and many a long moon since I read a literary magazine where the standard of the verse contributions was as consistently high as here." But *Akros* has also printed many young or unknown poets; as Hugh MacDiarmid said in the *Burns Chronicle:* "Glen is doing invaluable work not only in issuing volumes of poems and critical pamphlets but also in publishing *Akros* . . . He has, amongst other things, gathered round him and printed work by a whole group of younger poets, many of them writing in Scots." On the publication of no.12 an *Aberdeen Press and Journal* reviewer saw the magazine as "the most vigorous force in modern Scots poetry-making". Nos.13 and 14 were published together as special Hugh MacDiarmid issues and Tom Scott, writing in *Agenda*, said: "*Akros* has easily established itself as by far the best Scottish poetry magazine for decades: it has no rival in sight." But appreciation of the magazine has not been confined to Scottish critics: Peter Finch, in *Second Aeon*, saw it as "the Scottish giant thundering on covering the full Scots scene of poetry and criticism"; *Laissez Faire* saw it as having "established itself as one of the best magazines of our time"; and a *Littack* reviewer, writing on the publication of no.22 said: "one of the great literary magazines of these islands in the past ten years." The Scottish Arts Council have supported *Akros* with a grant since no.6. Despite this generous help, *Akros* remains dependent on healthy sales, and particularly on a healthy list of subscribers--personal subscribers and library subscribers. *The Library Review* kindly described *Akros* as "Scotland's most lively literary journal". A subscription is the cheapest and most convenient way to buy *Akros*--four issues (priced at 35p each) cost only £1.25 including postage paid in the U.K. Overseas subscriptions are £1.50. Send to: Akros Publications, 14 Parklands Avenue, Penwortham, Preston, Lancashire, PR1 OQL.

JOHN C. WESTON. *HUGH MACDIARMID'S "A DRUNK MAN LOOKS AT THE THISTLE". AN ESSAY*   Wrappers / £0.55
". . . very good value for the money. For a start nearly one thousand lines of the poem are given as quotations to illustrate Weston's description and explanation of the whole"--J.K. Annand, *Akros*.

ALEXANDER SCOTT. *THE MACDIARMID MAKARS 1923-1972. AN ESSAY*   Wrappers / £0.45
A thorough, knowledgeable and shrewd account of this important period in Scottish poetry.

DUNCAN GLEN. *THE INDIVIDUAL AND THE 20th-CENTURY SCOTTISH LITERARY TRADITION*   Paperback / £0.55
". . . principal commitment is to modern Scottish poetry . . . But he has much of importance to say about modern poetry in Europe and America"--Jeremy Hooker, *The Anglo-Welsh Review*.

ALEXANDER SCOTT. *CANTRIPS. POEMS*   Cloth / £1.13
"Will help confirm this poet's high reputation"--*The Glasgow Herald*.

ALASTAIR MACKIE. *CLYTACH. POEMS*
Cloth / £1.15   :   Paperback / £0.55
"Amongst the finest of living Scots poets"--Alexander Scott, *The Glasgow Review*.

MAURICE LINDSAY. *THIS BUSINESS OF LIVING. POEMS*
Cloth / £1.13
"The excellent qualities of vigour, directness, clarity and honesty"--*BBC Arts Review*.

Available, post paid in U.K., from
Akros Publications
14 Parklands Avenue, Penwortham, Preston
Lancashire, PR1 0QL